Henry James

AND THE

MASS

MARKET

MARCIA JACOBSON

The University of Alabama Press

*Publication of this book has been assisted by a grant
from the Auburn University Humanities Fund.*

The author acknowledges permission to reprint the
following in slightly revised form as Chapters Two,
Three, and Seven, respectively.

"Popular Fiction and Henry James's Unpopular
Bostonians," by Marcia Jacobson, *Modern Philology* 73
(February 1976), by permission of the University of
Chicago Press, copyright © 1976 by The University of
Chicago.

"Convention and Innovation in *The Princess Casamassima,*" by Marcia Jacobson, *Journal of English and
Germanic Philology* 76 (April 1977), by permission of
the University of Illinois Press, copyright © 1977 by
The Board of Trustees of the University of Illinois.

"Literary Convention and Social Criticism in Henry
James's *The Awkward Age,*" by Marcia Jacobson, *Philological Quarterly* 54 (Summer 1975), copyright © 1975
by *Philological Quarterly,* The University of Iowa.

Library of Congress Cataloging in Publication Data

Jacobson, Marcia Ann.
    Henry James and the mass market.

    Bibliography: p.
    Includes index.
    1. James, Henry, 1843–1916—Criticism and inter-
pretation. 2. James, Henry, 1843–1916—Authorship.
3. Authors and readers. 4. Books and reading—History—
19th century. I. Title.
PS2127.A9J32   1983   813'.4   82-17639
ISBN 0-8173-0145-3

To My Parents

I am not sure that Henry James had not secretly dreamed of being a "best seller" in the days when that odd form of literary fame was at its height; at any rate he certainly suffered all his life—and more and more as time went on—from the lack of recognition among the very readers who had most warmly welcomed his early novels.

—Edith Wharton, *A Backward Glance*

...I introduced [W. W.] Jacobs, whom Henry had never met. We sat and talked; suddenly James leant across and said, "Mr. Jacobs, I envy you." "You, Henry James, envy me!" cried Jacobs, always the most modest of men. James acknowledged the compliment with a graceful wave of the hand. "Ah, Mr. Jacobs," he said, "you are popular! Your admirable work is appreciated by a wide circle of readers; it has achieved popularity. Mine—never goes into a second edition. I should so much have loved to be popular!"

—Alfred Sutro, quoted in Simon Nowell-Smith,
The Legend of the Master

CONTENTS

ACKNOWLEDGMENTS

Reconstructing the context from which an author's work comes requires access to good libraries and uninterrupted time. I was fortunate in having both as I worked on *Henry James and the Mass Market*. The State Historical Society of Wisconsin and the University of Wisconsin, Madison, Memorial Library together provided a fine collection of nineteenth-century periodicals; the interlibrary loan staff at the Memorial Library was always helpful in locating now-forgotten novels; and the Chicago Public Library was kind enough to track down a couple of elusive magazines for me. The University of Wisconsin Graduate School Research Committee provided me with support for several summers, and the Institute for Research in the Humanities, University of Wisconsin, welcomed me into a most supportive community of scholars and gave me an uninterrupted year in which to work. It is a pleasure to record my thanks here.

I am also grateful to Auburn University for support from the Auburn Humanities Fund; to the *Journal of English and Germanic Philology, Modern Philology,* and *Philological Quarterly* who published early versions of three of my chapters and granted permission to reprint; and to Frances Henderson, Juanita Reese, and Wanda Schultz who typed the many drafts of my manuscript. And there are my friends and colleagues whose questions, suggestions, and encouragement made all the difference: Peter Brooks, James M. Cox, Frederick Crews, William M. Gibson, Merton M. Sealts, Jr., Dwight St. John, and William Veeder. I knew when I began that no scholar works alone; these readers taught me that a scholar's debts are not only to books.

A Note on Works Cited in the Text

References to *The Notebooks of Henry James,* ed. F. O. Matthiessen and Kenneth B. Murdock (1947; reprint, New York: Oxford University Press, 1961) are cited by the letter *N* followed by a page reference. References to James's fiction are to the New York Edition, *The Novels and Tales of Henry James,* 26 vols. (1907–17; reprint, New York: Scribner's, 1961–65). I have chosen to use this edition in preference to first edition texts because of its greater availability. Where a first edition text differs significantly, I have noted the fact.

Henry James

AND THE

MASS MARKET

ONE

The Literary Marketplace

Our usual image of Henry James is the one he left us with: James the Master, an aloof, self-sustained artist, governed by a devotion to style and a passion for form. It is the persona of the New York Edition prefaces, a persona that obscures another aspect of this complex author. The James who in 1883 turned his back on America after his parents' deaths to live in London for the next fifteen years is a very different figure. His letters and essays reflect an active interest in the turmoil of end-of-the-century English life. In 1884, James wrote Thomas Sergeant Perry: "nothing *lives* in England to-day but politics. They are all-devouring, & their mental uproar crowds everything out. This is more & more the case; we are evidently on the edge of an enormous political cycle, which will last heaven knows how long. I should hate it more if I didn't also find it interesting."[1] In "London" (1888; revised 1893), he commented on the equally interesting and distressing problems of the poor: official Westminster with its wealth and power is contrasted to nearby Green Park where "the unemployed lie thick on the grass and cover the benches with a brotherhood of greasy corduroys"—and of the rich: "The mind of Mayfair, when it aspires to show what it really can do, lives in the hope of a new divorce case, and an indulgent providence—

London is positively in certain ways the spoiled child of the world—abundantly recognizes this particular aptitude and humors the whim."[2] The same James who attentively examined social and political change was also reexamining the nature of his fiction. Even before *The Portrait of a Lady* (1881) was finished, he had written to Perry: "I mean…to 'quit' for awhile paying so much attention to the young unmarried American female— to stop, that is making her the central figure: which is of necessity a limitation."[3] After living in England for a while and observing and reflecting on English life, he insisted that the international contrast which had hitherto been the central theme of his fiction and which he had used to highlight the young unmarried American female had no relevance to what he had come to think of as real life. In 1888, he wrote to his brother William:

> For myself, at any rate, I am deadly weary of the whole "international" state of mind—so I *ache,* at times, with fatigue at the way it is constantly forced upon me as a sort of virtue or obligation. I can't look at the English-American world, or feel about them, any more, save as a big Anglo-Saxon total, destined to such an amount of melting together that an insistence on their differences becomes more and more idle and pedantic; and that the melting together will come the faster the more one takes it for granted…. Literature, fiction in particular, affords a magnificent arm for such taking for granted, and one may so do an excellent work with it. I have not the least hesitation in saying that I aspire to write in such a way that it would be impossible to an outsider to say whether I am at a given moment an American writing about England or an Englishman writing about America….[4]

James protests too much. Later, when the insecurities of his position as an outsider had diminished, he noted less defensively that fictional consideration of America no longer had any relevance to his own life; he had become too acclimatized to England to deal with America in his fiction. In 1890, he wrote to William Dean Howells: "One thing only is clear, that henceforth I must do, or half do, England in fiction—as the place I see most today, and, in a sort of way, know best. I have at least more acquired notions of it, on the whole, than of any other world, and it will serve as well as any other. It has been growing distincter that America fades from me, and as she never trusted me at best, I can trust *her*, for effect, no longer."[5]

And so, for the most part, he turned away from the international theme to try a new kind of fiction. With *The Bostonians* (1886), he broke with his past practice and dealt with a subject of current political interest—post–Civil War life in America. In writing the novel, he schooled himself in the art of writing topical fiction. As he became increasingly immersed in English life, he turned to contemporary English issues in his major works—the plight of the working class in *The Princess Casamassima* (1886), the aesthetic movement in *The Tragic Muse* (1890), contemporary London morals in *What Maisie Knew* (1897) and *The Awkward Age* (1899). As early as 1888, James described one impetus behind these works. Wearied by the long novels he had been writing, he announced to Robert Louis Stevenson that he would write only short pieces for a while, and then added: "I want to leave a multitude of pictures of my time, projecting my small circular frame upon as many different spots as possible and going in for number as well as quality, so that the number may constitute a total having a certain value as observation and testimony."[6]

Coincident with James's settling in London and seeking a new direction for his fiction was an immense change in the literary marketplace: the eighties and nineties saw the beginning of what we now term the mass market.[7] The causes and general results of this change are many. The eighties brought numerous changes in the production and distribution of books in both England and America. Costs dropped steadily as wood-pulp paper and high-speed printing were introduced. Cheap paper reprints of older fiction and, until the passage of the International Copyright Law in 1891, of contemporary foreign fiction were increasingly available. Numerous "libraries" of such books came into existence. Cheap reprints were offered as premiums with all sorts of merchandise. In England in 1885, George Moore published a new novel, *The Mummer's Wife,* in one inexpensive volume, thus imitating American practice and seriously challenging the English custom of publishing new books in expensive three-volume editions. More and more English books were issued in one volume in succeeding years, ultimately displacing the three-decker and in the process fatally weakening a lending library system that had depended on books too expensive for the consumer to buy himself. By the nineties, bookselling in both countries had become a big business, and the last decade of the century was marked by a proliferation of bookstores, publishing houses, and trade journals—and, of course, authors.

A new reading public in the two countries accompanied the increased availability of books. Population growth and a gradual change in the literacy rate as schooling became widespread through the century led to a dramatic increase in the absolute number of readers. With this increase, the proportion of middlebrow and lowbrow readers to highbrow readers altered drastically with the former far outnumbering the latter and so forming for the very first time a mass reading public. I am hesitant to say that such readers came from the newly educated lower and middle classes (the parallel equation of the upper classes and highbrow readers is patently absurd), but in fact many did, since these newly educated classes were often meagerly exposed to books and ideas. A generally improved standard of living gave more and more of these people money to buy books and leisure to read. It was a very different reading public from that which had nurtured the mid-century writers whom James had grown up reading and who inevitably stood as models for him. Dickens and Trollope had written for audiences that were considerably more homogeneous than that at the end of the century. Writers and readers came from a narrower cross-section of the population; the assaults on the economic and social order, family life, and religion that figure so prominently at the end of the century were barely present. A community of shared assumptions united writer and reader in a way no longer possible by the time James settled in England. Dickens and Trollope can justly be regarded as spokesmen of their times; certainly their readers thought of them as such. The situation in which James found himself was a grand exaggeration of that of mid-century America. The more diverse American culture had welcomed the great Victorian novelists and their lesser counterparts and had nourished a similar body of popular novelists; at the same time, in Hawthorne and Melville it produced two remarkable minority writers distinguished by an antagonistic relationship to the general culture. At the end of the century, the wider cross-section of readers meant a new diversity of interests competing in the marketplace, while the increase in middlebrow and lowbrow readers meant more weight massed against the minority writer. In this situation, the authority of the author as a spokesman for his whole culture was greatly diminished.

The coincidence of such changes made the emergence of the best seller as we know it inevitable. The enlarged, indiscriminate reading audience hungered for fiction that would entertainingly and reassuringly explain contemporary social change. The eighties and nineties consequently are distinguished in literary history by the extraordinary increase in the amount of topical fiction produced. The working-class novel, the feminist novel, the religious crisis novel all date from this period—as do the detective story and the exotic adventure novel, escapist fiction which is after all a form of response to social change. With the lowering of production costs and the increasing number of potential buyers, extremely large editions of such books as were judged to appeal widely were printed. And they sold. And sales inspired more sales. The phenomenon attracted attention. *The Oxford English Dictionary* gives 1899 as the year in which the term "best seller" first appeared, though it was not widely used until well after the turn of the century. Trade journals noted the interest in sales. When the *Book-man* appeared in London in 1891, it introduced in its first edition a column entitled "Sales of Books During the Month." This was a primitive best-seller list, based on information from a handful of bookstores, excluding reprints, cheap editions, and books sold by subscription. But the column reappeared every month and grew in comprehensiveness. In 1895 the first New York edition of the *Bookman* followed suit with lists of sales. James D. Hart, in *The Popular Book,* summarizes the relationship between this interest in sales and the new reading public of the period: "Certainly, the whole concept of best sellers accords with the increase in the book-buying public to the point where it represents a mass culture hesitant of its own taste and dependent upon the endorsement of the greatest number."[8]

In a discussion of the literary marketplace in the eighties and nineties, the term "best seller" thus has a special appropriateness. Yet it is not an entirely satisfactory term. Hart notes its limitations: "It indicates a superlative; it is used as a comparative. 'Best seller' means only a book that sells better than the general run of books in a given place during a given time. As a measurement of either quality or duration, it is open to question."[9] If we use the term to apply only to those books that appeared on the *Bookman's* lists, we do not make it more precise, for those lists were not accurate accounts of sales. The exclusion of certain types of books gives a distorted picture of the market. Mark Twain's books, for example, were sold by subscription and so never appear on lists of the period, yet he undoubtedly outsold many of the authors who were included. Publishers' statistics would probably yield a more accurate picture of the literary marketplace than the somewhat haphazard canvass of bookstores, but such statistics were not usually made public (certainly not in the case of pirated books) and today are simply lost with the disappearance of many of the old publishing houses and their records. The term "best seller" is most useful if we recognize its impreciseness and use it to include books and genres that we know from contemporary discussions sold particularly well.

Although the best seller is a characteristic feature of the eighties and nineties, the term is not so restricted that it cannot be applied to earlier books. One might point to *Uncle Tom's Cabin* as an early example of the phenomenon. But the book is just that: a phenomenon. The historical situation behind it gave it a topical appeal of intense but limited duration. The book itself was widely pirated and available in a variety of cheap editions; stage adaptations in effect advertised it; and it reached not only the usual mid-century readers of social novels but also readers who seldom read or bought fiction. We recognize a situation similar to that which recurred frequently at the end of the century. In the case of novels like Dickens's, however, the term "popular" is more appropriate, though this term too has its limitations. If we use the word accurately, we call a book popular when it speaks to and for the general public, when the plot and character conventions employed dramatize the shared assumptions of writer and reader. We pass no value judgment in using the term; obviously such books can vary greatly in quality and in acceptability to the public. A best seller is necessarily a popular book: it must appeal to the mass of readers, although given the diverse reading public in which it originates, it will rarely appeal to all classes of readers. But a popular book is not necessarily a best seller. Dickens's novels appealed to many, sold well, and continued to sell through the eighties and nineties. But they usually did not have the characteristics of the late-nineteenth-century best seller: topical appeal, large editions, and immediate but generally short-lived acclaim.

The change in the literary marketplace and in the reading public inspired debate among authors themselves as to the nature and purpose of their work. The majority, attuned to the mass market and its interests, cast the writer in the role of businessman with a commodity, his books, to sell. In *The Novel: What It Is* (1893), F. Marion Crawford, one of the consistent best sellers of the period, bluntly observes, "There are, I believe, two recognized ways of looking at art: art for the public or 'art for art,' to adopt the current French phrase. Might we not say, Art for the buyer and art for the seller?" To Crawford, only one of the two made sense. In his description of his work, fiction becomes a commodity that helps the public by providing it with entertainment and pleasurable instruction and by promoting social harmony. In writing such a work, the author appeals to the already established views of his audience, as Crawford's confident generalizations imply:

> We are nothing more than public amusers.... It is good to
> make people laugh; it is sometimes salutary to make them
> shed tears; it is best of all to make our readers think—not
> too serious thoughts, nor such as require an intimate
> knowledge of science and philosophy to be called thoughts
> at all—but to think, and, thinking, to see before them char-

acters whom they might really like to resemble, acting in
scenes in which they themselves would like to take a part....
     The foundation of good fiction and good poetry seems to
be ethic rather than aesthetic. Everything in either which
appeals to the taste, that is, to the aesthetic side, may ultimately perish as a mere matter of fashion; but that which
speaks to man as man, independently of his fashions, his
habits, and his tastes, must live and find a hearing with
humanity so long as humanity is human. The right understanding of men and women leads to the right relations of
men and women, and in this way, if in any, a novel may do
good; when written to attain this end, it may live....[10]

Walter Besant, another best-selling author and popularly
admired man of letters, expresses similar ideas in *The Art of
Fiction* (1884). There is less emphasis on the obligation to be
entertaining, but there is the same moral earnestness and
consent to established values, the same notion that the
reader can be taught without being required to think, and
the same ingratiating wish to see the novel improve social
relationships:

The modern novel converts abstract ideas into living models; it gives ideas, it strengthens faith, it preaches a higher
morality than is seen in the actual world; it commands the
emotions of pity, admiration, and terror; it creates and
keeps alive the sense of sympathy; it is the universal
teacher; it is the only book which the great mass of reading
mankind ever do read; it is the only way in which people
can learn what other men and women are like; it redeems
their lives from dulness, puts thoughts, desires, knowledge,
and even ambitions into their hearts: it teaches them to talk,
and enriches their speech with epigrams, anecdotes and
illustrations. It is an unfailing source of delight to millions,
happily not too critical....
     Again, the modern English novel, whatever form it takes,
almost always starts with a conscious moral purpose. When

it does not, so much are we accustomed to expect it, that one feels as if there has been a debasement of the Art.[11]

Using Besant's title as his own (also in 1884), James contributed to the debate by proposing a rather different notion of the art of fiction. He took issue with Besant's belief that there are specific rules that an aspiring writer should follow. Even more important, he disagreed with Besant's assumption that art is for the buyer; for James, art is for the seller, first and foremost: "A novel is in its broadest definition a personal impression of life; that, to begin with, constitutes its value, which is greater or less according to the intensity of the impression." Writing becomes a vocation instead of a business. Affording amusement or instruction becomes irrelevant as does facilitating social harmony. The only obligation the novelist has is that of conveying his unique vision of life as faithfully as possible: "the air of reality (solidity of specification) seems to me to be the supreme virtue of a novel—the merit in which all its other merits (including that conscious moral purpose of which Mr. Besant speaks) helplessly and submissively depend. If it be not there, they are all as nothing, and if these be there, they owe their effect to the success with which the author has produced the illusion of life. The cultivation of this success, the study of this exquisite process, form, to my taste, the beginning and the end of the art of the novelist." The "illusion of life," James continues, is created not merely from the author's actual experiences, but also from his impressions of the world around him: "Experience is...an immense sensibility, a kind of huge spider-web, of the finest silken threads, suspended in the chamber of consciousness and catching every air-bourne particle in its tissue. It is the very atmosphere of the mind...." In emphasizing the artist's perception, James has moved as far as possible from the notion of art as a commodity.

Yet "The Art of Fiction" is not therefore a modernist manifesto. The twentieth-century reader is struck by James's recognition of the subjectivity of experience and by his refusal to endorse the moralistic. At the same time, he must recognize that there is something very traditional about the essay. In granting the private vision of the artist so much importance, James is instinctively if not consciously restoring to the artist the authority which the mass market and its demands had taken from him. It is in consequence of this emphasis that James concludes his essay by addressing what he considers the "most interesting" issue that Besant raised: that of the writer's "conscious moral purpose." Far from discerning such a purpose in the contemporary English and American novel, James is struck by its lack of moral passion, by its "diffidence." His response is not to urge the novelist to more strenuous moralizing but to articulate what is implicit throughout his whole essay: "There is one point at which the moral sense and the artistic sense lie very near together; that is, in the light of the very obvious truth that the deepest quality of a work of art will always be the quality of the mind of the producer. In proportion as that mind is rich and noble will the novel, the picture, the statue, partake of the substance of beauty and truth"[12] — which is to say that a fine intelligence will perceive experience in moral terms. This is not the pronouncement of the lesser writer for whom moralizing comes easier than a moral vision of life, nor is it that of the modernist who doubts the universal validity of his own vision. Instead, it is an attitude that allies James with his great Victorian predecessors and accounts for his persistent attempt to dramatize moral issues in his fiction.[13]

Whereas James's "Art of Fiction" has been analyzed in light of its cultural context,[14] the same kind of attention has not been paid to the fiction he wrote during his London years—although the coincidence of his search for new ma-

terial and the development of the mass market suggest a
need for such study. Both biographers and critics tend to
divide the period into two segments decisively separated by
James's attempt to write for the stage; neither group pays
more than passing attention to James's interaction with the
mass market. Leon Edel, Maxwell Geismar, Edmund Wilson, and, to a lesser extent, F. W. Dupee all see the novels of
the eighties as James's not entirely successful effort to deal
with large social concerns and the work of the nineties as
symptomatic of a regressive self-absorption. Oscar Cargill
and Sergio Perosa discuss James's French-inspired Naturalism in the eighties and his various experimental techniques
in the nineties. Lyall Powers treats only the novels of the
eighties and considers them in the context of French Naturalism. Walter Isle and Joseph Wiesenfarth treat the fiction
of the nineties and look at the ways in which James's experience with the drama altered his handling of the novel. Donald David Stone, in an apparent exception to the trend,
treats James in the context of the historic changes of the
eighties—but he too accepts the notion that the work of the
nineties is best understood as experimental in nature. He
looks only at the work of the eighties and argues that James
responded to the historic changes of the period by directing
his attention inward and away from social life.[15]

There is certainly evidence to support all these approaches in their general outlines. But it is also clear that
when James studies have transcended New Critical analy-
ses, they have been dominated by psychological criticism
and a rather loose historicism. William Stafford and Adeline Tinter in their recent surveys of James criticism have
applauded the relatively few efforts to place James in his
cultural context and have urged more work in this direction.[16] But one barely touched area of contextual study remains that of James's relation to the popular market. I
offer this book as such a study. My obligations differ from

those of the critic who would write a source study. He must prove that his subject read and drew upon a given work in creating his own. My task is to describe the context within which James was working by identifying its distinguishing features and to show that he had opportunity to recognize it sufficiently to have been influenced. Since, to anticipate, I will be treating James's works as adaptations of a variety of best-selling genres, this means showing that he would have had ample opportunity to read or hear of enough examples of each genre he was interested in to be able to isolate its particular form and conventions. The people he knew, the magazines he read, and the articles he wrote provide the basic material for reconstructing the context within which he worked. Although an artist may not always be fully conscious of the influence exerted by his literary context, I am inclined to believe that a writer as sensitive to the marketplace as James was fully aware of this aspect of his work. Our awareness, in turn, enhances our understanding of both the writer and his fiction.

The James who feared failure and who longed from his youth to be a great man frequently presents himself as above the popular market with its power to canonize and enrich a writer it loved and condemn to oblivion one it did not. In his public accounting of the origins of his fiction in the New York Edition prefaces, James rarely cites ephemeral contemporary fiction as an influence, acknowledging instead the inspiration of a writer of established status, a personal experience, or an intriguing technical problem. When addressing the readers of the *Century* (in "Du Maurier and London Society," 1883), he freely expressed his contempt for British aesthetic sensibility: "They [the English] have not a spontaneous artistic life; their taste is a matter of conscience, reflection, duty, and the writer who in our time has appealed to them most eloquently on behalf of art has rested his plea on moral standards of right and wrong. It is impossible to live much among them, to be a spectator of their habits, their manners, their arrangements, without perceiving that the artistic point of view is the last that they naturally take."[17] In "The Next Time" (1895), a tale of literary life written after several years of commercial failures, the period is sweepingly condemned as "the age of trash triumphant" (XV, 159).

But James's attitudes are never simple. When he spoke as the Master, the American abroad, or the minority artist, a part of himself remained silent. William Veeder has recently emphasized the young Henry James's extensive knowledge of popular fiction in showing that James began with a literary style and mode of characterization very similar to that of currently popular writers and evolved a distinctly personal way of using language by the time of *The Portrait of a Lady* (1881).[18] Having achieved this, James did not lose interest in popular fiction. He was an inveterate newspaper and magazine reader and would have read contemporary serializations and book reviews (and sometimes seen himself seriously compared to such writers as Crawford or Frank Stockton). He still occasionally reviewed current fiction as he had done at the beginning of his career. Many of his friends and acquaintances were extraordinarily successful with the new mass market: E. F. Benson, Frances Hodgson Burnett, F. Marion Crawford, Rudyard Kipling, Robert Louis Stevenson, and Mrs. Humphry Ward all wrote best sellers. Scattered references in his notebooks and letters indicate familiarity with other best-selling authors as well. For all of James's scorn, he maintained a strong interest in the popular market in England and America.

Surrounded as he was by successful friends who were enjoying both fame and fortune, it is not surprising that James, too, dreamt of benefiting from the mass market.[19]

He had some reason to be sanguine. "Daisy Miller" (1878) had brought him notoriety, if not money. In 1883, Macmillan had published a fourteen-volume collected edition of his work. Periodicals had begun to refer to him as a leading figure in American letters. When James published "The Art of Fiction" in the thoroughly middlebrow *Longman's*, he made plain his hopes. By speaking in opposition to Besant (who, incidentally, was a frequent contributor to *Longman's*), James presented himself as a rival for public attention, that is, as one who would compete in the same field with the hope of excelling. He spoke, as we have seen, with an authority more akin to that of his Victorian predecessors than of his peers in the eighties. Earlier audiences, he knew, had responded to Dickens and Thackeray; he must have believed that the contemporary middlebrow reader, if given a chance, would still respond to such a voice and such a vision rather than to the author who sought simply to ingratiate himself with the majority of the public. It is an attitude that translates into repeated attempts to work within the best-selling genres of the period in a way that would yield a probing examination of the society that gave them birth.

If we are tempted to charge James with naiveté in appraising the reading public and so overestimating his chances for popular success, we must remember that the mass market was unprecedented. Even Crawford, who so accurately aimed his fiction and his theorizing at it, was unable to account for it. In *The Novel: What It Is* he observed, "The point upon which people differ is the artistic one, and the fact that such differences of opinion exist makes it possible that two writers as widely separated as Mr. Henry James and Mr. Rider Haggard, for instance, find appreciative readers in the same year of the same century—a fact which the literary history of the future will find it hard to explain."[20] We find it easier to explain than he thought but only because time has granted us a perspective that he and James lacked. Like Crawford, James had difficulty grasping the extent of diversity in the late-nineteenth-century reading audience. Ignorant of this, he could not foresee that his refusal to play the roles of entertainer and moralizer would cut him off from a wide spectrum of readers.

Examination of James's work in its fictional context will show how James used the conventions of contemporary fiction to appeal to his society at the same time as he examined it. For now, a handful of letters provides a capsule summary of James's encounter with the mass market. He initially believed he could compete successfully in the marketplace. With some embarrassment and much hope he wrote to Thomas Bailey Aldrich to negotiate the publication of the not yet completed *Princess Casamassima* in the *Atlantic*:

> the *Century* is to publish, de moi, 1/ a story in three parts. 2/ a story in two parts. 3/ a story in six parts [*The Bostonians*], and three or four short tales, from my turning hand are to appear (this is a profound secret)—have been, in a word, secured, *à prix d'or* in—je vous en donne en milles—the New York Sunday *Sun!* This last fact, I repeat, is really as yet *a complete and sacred secret.* Please bury it in oblivion and burn my letter. I mention it, with the preceding items, simply to denote that by July 1865 [*sic*: he means 1885] I expect to be in the enjoyment of a popularity which will require me to ask $500 a number for the successive instalments of *The Princess Casamassima....*[21]

James's embarrassment at publishing in the rather lowbrow *Sun* did not stop him from doing so. But the popularity he hoped such publication would contribute to never came; both *The Bostonians* and *The Princess* were commercial failures. Each of these novels had evidently been a calculated appeal to the marketplace, for in 1888 a bewildered James wrote to Howells, "I have entered upon evil days.... I am still staggering a good deal under the mysterious and (to me) inexplicable injury wrought—apparently upon my situation by my last two novels, the *Bostonians* and the *Princess,* from which I expected so much and derived so little. They have reduced the desire, and the demand for my productions to zero...."[22] The same note of bewilderment appears in his comments in the preface of the New York Edition of *The Tragic Muse* as he recounts the commercial failure of that novel too (see VII, vi). James may well have prided himself on using the conventions of the best seller to produce a better novel than his competitors had, but he obviously also wanted his books to sell. So he intensified his assault on the public by turning to the theater, a move which anyone who believes that James gracefully accepted his role as a minority writer must be hard pressed to explain. He covered his embarrassed eagerness by insisting that necessity lay behind his new endeavor, though there is no evidence to confirm this. Writing to William James in 1890, he even coyly refused to name what he was about, referring to his work as "The matter you expressed a friendly hope about the success of, and which for all sorts of reasons I desire to be extremely secret, silent and mysterious about—I mean the enterprise I covertly mentioned to you as conceived by me with a religious and deliberate view of gain over the greater scale than the Book (my Books at least) can ever approach bringing to me...."[23]

It took the spectacular theatrical failure to destroy James's illusions. Several weeks after being booed on the opening night of *Guy Domville* (1895), James wrote Howells: "I *have* felt, for a long time past, that I have fallen upon evil days, every sign or symbol of one's being in the least *wanted,* anywhere or by any one, having so utterly failed. A new generation, that I know not, and mainly prize not, has taken universal possession. The sense of being utterly out of it weighed me down, and I asked myself what the future would be."[24] Seven years earlier, James had also written to Howells that he had "entered upon evil days," but then he could not explain why his novels had failed to find favor. Now, in acknowledging a new generation, he acknowledged the mass market.

After this, James adopted an attitude of apparent indifference to popular opinion. In the preface to the New York Edition of *The Awkward Age,* he recalls his publisher's telling him that the novel was doing badly, and he shrugs off this fact to recall instead the fun he had writing the book (IX, xv–xvi). The pose often governed his private life too. In 1899 he wrote to Howard Sturgis: "I greatly applaud the tact with which you tell me that scarce a human being will understand a word, or an intention, or an artistic element or glimmer of any sort, of my book [*The Awkward Age*]. I tell *myself*—and the 'reviews' tell me—such truths in much cruder fashion. But it's an old, old story—and if I 'minded' now as much as I once did, I should be well beneath the Sod."[25] Yet James continued to turn his hand to best-selling genres as long as he lived in London, adapting them to provide a means of analyzing and criticizing contemporary life. If he no longer expected to win a popular following, and there is no evidence that he did, he accepted the role of minority writer with reluctance. In 1890, after the publication and evident failure of *The Tragic Muse,* he had written William: "One must go one's way and know what one's about and have a general plan and a private religion—in short have made up one's mind as to *ce qui en est* with a public draggling after which simply leads one in the gutter. One has always a 'public' enough if one has an audible vibration—even if it should only come from one's self. I shall never make my fortune—nor anything like it; but—I know what I shall do, and it won't be bad."[26] We recognize this as "The Art of Fiction" translated into advice for living so that art is a vocation undertaken in the service of the artist himself. In 1890, it was mere bravado; only at the end of the decade was it a way of life.

TWO

The Bostonians

The Bostonians is James's farewell to America. He returned
to visit his family in Cambridge late in October of 1881 and
although delighted with the hospitality of his family and
friends was soon longing to return to England. At the end
of November, he entered in his notebook a long evaluation
of his recent years in London. He dwelt lovingly on the
social and literary successes he had enjoyed, and observed
about the present, "Heaven forgive me! I feel as if my time
were terribly wasted here!" (*N,* p. 24). He wrote to Grace
Norton that he intended to stay in America only until late
February, and "then I depart, *never again to return!*"[1] But his
mother died unexpectedly at the end of January, and James
stayed on until May. His return to Europe was short-lived;
in December of 1882 he was back in America again. He had
received word that his father was dying, and although he
arrived too late to see him before his death, he remained in
America until August of the next year to serve as his father's
executor and to be with his family. In the course of both
visits, James saw friends in New York and Washington and
thereby gained a sense of national life that extended beyond Boston and Cambridge. But his warm memories of
England and the loss of both parents with the undesired
extended visits that followed inevitably colored his Ameri-

can experience. He found much that was interesting, but little that was truly congenial, and when he finally returned to England, it was with a sense of real relief.[2] It is not surprising that *The Bostonians,* a novel that comes out of this period, should be a critical appraisal of American life.

James began thinking about *The Bostonians* while he was staying in Boston in 1883. He copied into his notebook the letter outlining the novel that he sent to J. R. Osgood, the publisher and literary agent who would bring it out in book form after magazine serialization. The novel was to deal with the feminist movement in Boston in the 1870s. In his earlier story, "The Point of View" (1882), James had glanced briefly at the cultural enthusiasms of Boston ladies and the social abandonment of American women in general by the money-making sex ("People have no time for making love; the men in particular are extremely busy" [XIV, 567]). Now he was returning to those women and studying them more extensively in the particular light of Boston in the 1870s. Yet James did not think of his subject as provincial or limited. After outlining his plot, he noted the representative quality of the proposed work: "I wished to write a very *American* tale, a tale very characteristic of our social conditions, and I asked myself what was the most salient and peculiar point in our social life. The answer was: the situation of women, the decline of the sentiment of sex, the agitation on their behalf" (*N*, p. 47). Boston and the feminist movement were only the starting point for a larger commentary on America.

One way in which James enlarged the range of his novel was by incorporating the themes of mesmerism and spiritualism into his presentation of the woman's rights movement. Many critics have noted the similarities between *The Bostonians* and two earlier books James knew: Hawthorne's *The Blithedale Romance* (1853) and Howells's *The Undiscovered Country* (1880). The trance-speaking Verena Tarrant, her mesmerist father, and her skeptical suitor all number among their immediate prototypes the main characters of Howells's novel. But Howells's central concern in *The Undiscovered Country* was the quest for spiritual certainty in an increasingly skeptical age; by associating Verena with the woman's movement, James was treating spiritualism as one of the many "crank" movements of the nineteenth century that prospered most conspicuously in the company of other, more respectable movements. In handling spiritualism this way, James's work is closer to Hawthorne's encompassing critique of his age. Howard Kerr in a discussion of *The Bostonians* in the context of nineteenth-century spiritualism notes James's firsthand acquaintance with the milieu he deals with and observes that the *The Bostonians* resembles "the anti-spiritualistic, anti-reform satires and magnetic romances of the 1850's"—two genres wedded in *The Blithedale Romance* and a number of lesser mid-century novels—even more than it does Howells's novel.[3] Seen this way, *The Bostonians* achieves its breadth in part through its contemporary reference (James's experience, Howells's novel) and in larger part through its invocation of a distinct American literary tradition.

James's larger incorporating theme, the feminist movement, seems a more puzzling choice at first glance. Although he had been interested in the problems of women from the beginning of his career, he knew relatively little about the feminist movement itself, as he was to confess when he finished the novel.[4] This lack of actual knowledge is readily apparent. Several critics have suggested real-life prototypes for Verena,[5] but these suggestions testify to James's grasp of one type of political personality, not to his understanding of the political movement itself. Accordingly, although James's feminists express a variety of viewpoints—most of them actually voiced by women of the 1870s—this variety is an aspect of characterization only.

James seems to have no sense of how dissension frag-
mented and weakened the movement. His feminists somehow work together, taking in all shades of belief; their
historical sisters found they could not, and the movement
split along conservative (Boston based) and radical (New
York and Western) lines, the former urging merely suffrage,
the latter this and much else, from dress reform to– occasionally–free love.

But if we accept the notion, implicit in James's letters,
that *The Bostonians* was intended to compete in the mass
market, the choice of subject matter is at once understandable. *The Bostonians* was conceived just after feminist fiction
began to appear. Unhappy wives and ambitious women
have always figured in fiction—one thinks of *Middlemarch*
and *The Portrait of a Lady,* or even of *Moll Flanders* and *Vanity
Fair*—but in the eighties a new kind of heroine appears,
sometimes incorporating these earlier roles but always differing from her predecessors, as my discussion will indicate,
in her awareness, or at least her creator's awareness, of the
changing role of women in society. She knows that new
careers are open to her, that she can and should have political opinions, and—though less often—that marriage is not
the only means to fulfillment. In short, a desire to define
and satisfy herself rather than to be useful or proper or
important characterizes her and separates her from previous literary heroines. She appears primarily in American
fiction in the eighties—lagging slightly behind actual historical change—and then in increasingly larger numbers in
both American and English fiction in the nineties. James
acknowledged the New Woman's American debut in "The
Chaperon" (1891), when Rose Tramore is faced with social
ostracism as a result of living with her *déclassée* mother: "It
was not too much to say that during this first winter of
Rose's heroic campaign [on behalf of her mother] she had
no communication whatever with the world. It had the ef-

fect of making her take to reading the new American books: she wanted to see how girls got on by themselves" (X, 470). In writing *The Bostonians,* James would be contributing to the newly emerging topical genre. As the feminist novel dealt with contemporary social history and as it was attracting increasing amounts of popular attention, it must have seemed an attractive vehicle for James's projected study of "our social conditions."

James himself has suggested a rather different impulse behind his desire to write a novel documenting social conditions. After copying the letter to Osgood outlining *The Bostonians,* he noted, "Daudet's *Évangéliste* has given me the idea of this thing" (*N*, p. 47). One might argue that James's study of Boston and New York life is roughly equivalent to the French Naturalists' examination of Paris. Yet critics have been reluctant to attribute much to the particular influence of Daudet's novel, for it resembles James's only in its general outline.[6] Daudet's book appeared early in 1883 and is a study in morbid psychology. It tells the story of the leader of a fanatical and feminist Protestant group and her conversion of a younger girl who subsequently abandons both her mother and her fiancé to take up life as an evangelist. The skeleton of James's novel is there: a young, sweet-tempered girl comes under the unhealthy influence of a stern, powerful woman and a radical and unappealing feminist group. But the American setting and the basic romance plot of James's novel suggest that this influence is as secondary as that of the antispiritualist satire. We can account more satisfactorily for James's book if we consider the influence of the contemporary feminist novel and another popular contemporary American genre: the Civil War romance.

James's novel itself implies knowledge of and indebtedness to the feminist novel in several ways. Toward the end of *The Bostonians,* the volatile Verena Tarrant is scheduled to speak on the Woman Question; her suitor, Basil Ransom, intervenes, and she never does give the speech. Instead, she leaves the woman's movement—and in doing so abandons all her professions of independence—and agrees to marry Ransom. The title of the proposed speech is the ironic title of a Howells novel—*A Woman's Reason* (1883)—which also portrays a heroine who is more emotional than logical and who finds that she cannot manage as an independent woman. While there are major differences between the two books (James's concerns are more political; Howells is concerned with the way his heroine's family life and social background have unfitted her for maturity), it is unlikely that James's echo of Howells's title, used as ironically as Howells himself used it, is coincidental. James's friendship with Howells and the fact that *A Woman's Reason* was running serially in the *Century* (February to October, 1883) when James was publishing there argue for his having read the book, as does his mention of it in the essay he wrote on Howells for *Harper's Weekly* (19 June 1886) shortly after finishing *The Bostonians*.

In addition to knowing *A Woman's Reason,* James must also have been aware of a more common type of New Woman novel: the story of the lady doctor. Medicine was one of the first professions to open up to women after the Civil War, and this fact was reflected in the appearance of lady doctor novels in the early eighties. Howells's *Dr. Breen's Practice* (1881) was one of the first. James read the novel as it appeared serially in the *Atlantic Monthly* (August to December) and wrote to Howells praising it.[7] This novel too is mentioned briefly in the essay on Howells. Other examples of the lady doctor novel are Elizabeth Stuart Phelps's *Doctor Zay,* which was serialized in the *Atlantic* in 1882 (April to September), and Sarah Orne Jewett's *A Country Doctor,* which was reviewed in the same magazine in September 1884. It is likely that James's desire to keep up with what the *Atlantic* was publishing and his watching for his own material to appear (a frequent occurrence in the early eighties) would have given him at least a cursory acquaintance with these books.

While these three novels differ in details, there are basic similarities among them. Although the emergence of the New Woman in the 1870s was the result of immense social changes after the Civil War, none of the New Woman novels presents very much of a context for its heroine. The plots are all similar: in each, a very attractive, even charismatic, heroine pursues a career for a while and then is challenged by a proposal of marriage; two of the three accept. In handling the career-versus-marriage theme, none of the authors examines the choice of a career with complete objectivity. In each case, external causes help the heroine choose. Howells's novel is the subtlest and most interesting of the three. His heroine, Grace Breen, undertook the study of medicine, which she found morally admirable but practically distasteful, to punish herself for failing to win the man she loved. When she fails to cure a patient, she again punishes herself, this time by marrying. Her choice of a mode of life is made at the behest of her perverse psychology, not as a result of an evaluation of the two alternatives. In the cases of Phelps and Jewett, the failure to let the claims of a career speak out is again evident—even though both authors theoretically endorse the idea of a career for a woman. Phelps's Dr. Zay is a brilliant physician, passionately dedicated to her work, convinced she should not marry. But near the end of the book, she suffers from diphtheria— after years of vibrant health—and so becomes a weak woman who can go on to become a properly dependent wife. Phelps is unable to trust what she and her heroine have said about the necessity of work. Jewett's Nan Prince, on the other hand, chooses a career in spite of being tempted by the prospect of marriage. But even here, the choice is an ambiguous endorsement of a career; Nan is afraid of marriage because she might transmit to her children her mother's tendency to alcoholism and madness.

James's incorporation of Mary Prance in *The Bostonians* is a tacit acknowledgment of the lady doctor novel, and his plot—a pretty girl torn between marriage and the woman's movement chooses marriage—is a variant of the career-versus-marriage theme. In both instances, we see James working within and against prevailing fictional conventions. Mary Prance is a doctor, but James's characterization of her—a brusque manner of speech, a boyish if not asexual deportment—suggests his impatience with the sentimentalizations of popular fiction (as well, unfortunately, as an all too common male conception of the professional woman). His handling of the career-versus-marriage theme indicates another kind of reservation about the popular genre. Unlike her fictional predecessors, Verena Tarrant is not asked to choose simply between a career and marriage; instead, she is asked to choose between the woman's movement *and* her domineering friend and mentor in the movement, Olive Chancellor, on one hand, and Basil Ransom, who despises the movement, on the other. What James has done, in essence, is to tell the old story of the young girl importuned by two suitors, while maintaining the appearance of a contemporary, topical plot. By doing this, James, like his predecessors, creates a way to avoid dispassionate consideration of the claims of a career for women. Because commitment to the movement means acceding to Olive's demand for an exclusive, perhaps lesbian, relationship, Verena must ultimately turn against her if she is to lead a normal life.[8] Whatever merits the woman's movement itself might have are irrelevant to Verena as she finally makes her choice. This kind of obfuscation was no doubt congenial to James given his conservatism and his limited knowledge of the movement. More important, the substitution of the two-suitor plot for the career-versus-marriage plot gave James characters who would stand for the competing values in the novel—and hence, in their confrontations, the basis for a more dramatic novel than the sort of thing Phelps and Jewett had produced.

This sense of dramatic opposition is at work everywhere in *The Bostonians*. In offering us a panoramic picture of the America he studied during his visits home, James paints a brilliant and often witty picture of a conflict-ridden nation, an America in which the Civil War has not yet ended.[9] In Boston itself the old-fashioned democratic humanitarianism of Miss Birdseye contrasts with the modern self-seeking ideas of Olive Chancellor and Mrs. Farrinder. Boston and New York appear as rivals for cultural dominance. Basil Ransom, a refugee from Mississippi who has come to New York, introduces the themes of conflict between North and South, republican and aristocratic manners, liberal and conservative philosophies. And most pervasive of all is the conflict signaled by the rival suitors, the conflict of male and female. While James portrays Miss Birdseye as having traded the abolitionist movement for the feminist movement, he does not consider her case as widely representative—although, in fact, many women followed the same route she had and after the war insisted that discussion of votes for Negroes necessarily entailed discussion of votes for women. Instead, he treats the feminist movement as a response to a perceived failure of masculinity in New England after the war, and therefore as an occasion for the expression of feminine anger at the betraying or disappointing male. There is some truth in this view. The loss of men from the North during the war was very heavy—a fact which James suggested in "A New England Winter" (1884) and which he implies in *The Bostonians* by showing us a Boston where the few men who remain are effete or ineffectual. Given this situation, the sex-denying responses of James's feminists are understandable. Mrs. Farrinder campaigns for suffrage and temperance in an effort to wrest political and social power from incompetent men like her husband, Dr. Prance acts as if there is only one sex and that of neuter gender, and Olive Chancellor nurses a pathological hatred of men and at the same time envies them and so dreams of giving herself up as a martyr to a great cause just as her brothers gave their lives in the war. In evoking these broad social conflicts, James breaks with his own past practice as a novelist. He also provides a context for his feminist concerns that at once makes his novel a more profound and more interesting work than anything his predecessors in the genre had done and at the same time evokes such stark oppositions that his New Woman's choice of marriage cannot bridge them to bring the harmony we conventionally expect at the end of a love story.

In broadening the scope of his novel in this way, James was acting in accord with the hint in his notebook postscript to a letter to Osgood: he was making his novel a commentary on America as a whole. But more than his desire to turn his recent visits home into literary material was at work in the way in which this aim took shape. When James first outlined his novel, he proposed that Ransom should be a "distant relative" (*N*, p. 47) of Olive, who had spent ten years in the West before his arrival in Boston. However, when James came to write the novel, he made Ransom a Mississippian and a Civil War veteran. The change brought a Southerner into contact with Northern life and, in addition to enriching James's picture of post–Civil War Boston, also constituted another appeal to the mass market by allying *The Bostonians* with the ever-increasing number of novels dealing with the Civil War and its aftermath that appeared after Reconstruction and reached the level of a best-selling genre by the mid-eighties.[10] Herbert Smith and Michael Peinovich have suggested that this change was urged on James by the *Century* when it agreed to serialize *The Bosto-*

nians.[11] It was an alteration that would add to the topical
appeal of the novel, and whether the idea originated with
the magazine or the author—its source is not clear—it must
have presented itself as an attractive idea to an author eager
to attract popular attention.

The "official" mood of the eighties was reconciliatory.
Both the *Atlantic* and the *Century* ran numerous articles on
the pre- and post-war South and on Civil War battles and
generals, the purpose being to educate the generation that
had grown up after the war and to soften the hearts of
those who had lived through it.[12] Civil War fiction, strongly
partisan during and immediately after the war, then quies-
cent during Reconstruction, emerged now as an additional
force for reconciliation—hence the possibility that the *Century* urged James to incorporate a Southerner. John William
De Forest's *Miss Ravenel's Conversion* (1867), with its strong
Union bias, is representative of early Civil War fiction—a
literature which transmuted the war into a conflict between,
as William Wasserstrom puts it, "hot Southern sinners and
cold Northern saints."[13] By the eighties, however, regional
sympathies and stereotypes were carefully modulated. The
most common form of these new Civil War novels was that
of the romance between a Northerner and a Southerner
who overcame their wartime prejudices and married, symbolically reuniting the Union. Often, one of the steps toward reconciliation was a recognition by the soldier suitor
that his opponents, the soldiers who fought for his loved
one's side, were as heroic as his own men had been. James
used both these conventions with significant variations in
The Bostonians.

James very likely had a firsthand acquaintance with the
genre. His friend Constance Fenimore Woolson's collection
of short stories, *Rodman the Keeper* (1880), includes as its title
story a tale in which a Northern and a Southern soldier
come to respect and depend upon one another, and another

story, "Old Gardiston," in which a Northern soldier successfully courts a Southern girl. In view of its date of composition, James probably read Woolson's book before writing *The Bostonians*; he praised it later in his essay on Woolson in *Harper's Weekly* in 1887 (12 February). Another work James may have known is S. Weir Mitchell's novel *In War-Time*, which was serialized in the *Atlantic* in 1884 (January to December) when James himself was frequently publishing there and certainly would have been looking at the magazine. This novel includes a subplot which details the romance between a Northern soldier and a Southern girl, in this case given special significance as a reconciliatory act by the fact that the girl's father, a Confederate captain, died believing that the boy's father, a Northern major, had inflicted his fatal wounds at Gettysburg. In addition, there was the work of such popular writers as Charles King and E. P. Roe. James may well have heard of or perhaps even looked at books like King's *Kitty's Conquest* (1884) and Roe's *His Sombre Rivals* (1883) and *An Original Belle* (1885), all three of which involve homage to the other side and a reconciliatory marriage. In 1889, when James reviewed military novels for his series on American letters for *Literature* (28 May), he included one of King's books, a fact that suggests that King was not totally unknown to fairly sophisticated readers, and Roe's books were always heavily advertised and widely read.

There is one additional but indirect way in which James was exposed to the conventions of the Civil War romance. In 1880, Henry Adams published anonymously a semisatirical account of American political life, a novel ironically called *Democracy*. The book cannot really be considered a Civil War novel because it is not centered upon the war or its immediate aftermath. But like *The Bostonians*, it includes some of the conventions found in the Civil War novel. One of the male characters is a Southern Civil War veteran (who,

like Basil Ransom, practices law and has an impoverished
mother and sisters dependent upon him) who courts (too
passively, it turns out) a Northern lady; at one point in the
novel, he visits Arlington Cemetery with the lady's sister
and talks to her about the war, helping her to understand
that both sides had their heroes. James read *Democracy* and
was sufficiently impressed by it to remark to Thomas Sergeant Perry, "It is good enough to make it a pity it isn't
better."[14] James's own short story "Pandora" (1884) reworks
some of the themes and episodes of *Democracy*. While "Pandora" can hardly be considered an attempt to improve on
Adams, it does testify to the impression Adams's novel had
on James. The similarities between Ransom and Adams's
Southern veteran suggest the same thing.

In the Civil War romance the soldier suitor is usually, but
not always, a Northerner, the girl a Southerner. This is apparently a tacit recognition of the Northern victory in the
war and an acknowledgment of the proverbial beauty of the
Southern belle. At the same time, the reconciliatory fiction
of the eighties does not insist upon sectional differences;
marriage to a Northerner is not, as Lillie Ravenel's was, a
conversion to the male point of view. Roe's *An Original Belle,*
for example, concludes with a Southern girl accepting a
Union soldier's hand and hazarding, "the North has con-
quered again." He silences her, however: "let us begin right.
For us there is no North or South. We are one for time, and
I trust for eternity."[15] Since James began his book with the
idea of writing about the Boston feminist movement, he
was constrained to make his male protagonist a Southerner
once he had decided to incorporate elements of the Civil
War novel into his book. His decision to cast his novel in
terms of a conflict between rival suitors made for a further
constraint: he would have to emphasize regional differences
in order to articulate the rivalry. Both constraints meant
that his book would be closer in texture to the impassioned,

partisan Civil War novel of the sixties than to the moderating novel of the eighties, and this result was clearly congenial to James.[16] The dramatic impact that he had gained in turning to the rival suitors would be reinforced by the evocation of sectional rivalry. This meant that regional differences could be legitimately emphasized, and James's perception of the divisiveness of American life would find vivid expression; it also meant that a conservative, antireformist point of view would win out in the struggle for Verena, and James's distaste for the woman's movement would be articulated. In superimposing the Civil War romance on the feminist novel, James had found the perfect vehicle for the expression of his ideas. He would be combining two popular genres to express unpopular ideas—a real risk for an author who sought a wide readership and one that James did nothing to lessen, for he exploited his critical opportunities as much as possible.

Regional differences are carefully emphasized. Ransom is specified not merely as a Southerner but as a Mississippian. This origin implies that his veneer of civilization is rather thin, Mississippi being only one step removed from the frontier at the time of the war.[17] And this indeed is the case. His chivalry thinly masks an aggressive sexuality, hinted at by his "leonine" hair and "sultry" accent;[18] it is not surprising that he virtually abducts Verena at the end of the novel. Being a Mississippian also means that he does not hold the patriarchal and elitist views of the pre–Civil War Southerner with the ease which the long-established plantation owner might. The stridency and overinsistence with which he expresses his views to Verena show him to be a man who is constantly proving himself. His social insecurity as well as his sexual arrogance are evident in his perpetual harangues. He typically declaims, "The whole generation is womanized; the masculine tone is passing out of the world; it's a feminine, a nervous, hysterical, chattering, canting age, an

age of hollow phrases and false delicacy and exaggerated
solicitudes and coddled sensibilities, which, if we don't look
out, will usher in the reign of mediocrity, of the feeblest
and flattest and the most pretentious that has ever been"
(p. 343), only to give himself away unawares.

Ransom also conforms to the general Southern type in
his lack of business acumen: though he claims to be an
ambitious man, he does not have the shrewdness requisite
to making a living as a lawyer in New York. In a moment of
insight, after being cheated by a business partner and losing
a number of clients on his own, he recognizes that his origin
and his love for abstract social and political issues are not
conducive to success: "he began to wonder whether there
were not a prejudice against his Southern complexion. Perhaps they didn't like the way he spoke.... He wondered
whether he were stupid and unskilled, and he was finally
obliged to confess to himself that he was unpractical"
(p. 192). He spends his days dreaming of leading a public
life but at the same time recognizes that he could never get
himself elected. It is entirely characteristic that he contem-
plates (albeit briefly) advancing himself by marriage—to
Olive, before he knows her, and later to her sister, Mrs.
Luna. On some level Ransom realizes that if he cannot
successfully play the role of businessman, he has the requi-
sites for the role of Southern charmer.

Verena and Olive similarly are presented as regional
types. Although Olive's fear and hatred of men seem to be
pathological, we look in vain for an account of the source of
her malaise. Such an explanation would enable us to see her
in terms of her private history and would trivialize her as a
representative character. Without it, she is simply given as a
type of Bostonian—and the type is readily identifiable. Her
rectitude, her moral earnestness, her austerity of manner,
and above all her delight in suffering and her belief in its
salutary effects—"the prospect of suffering was always, spir-

itually speaking, so much cash in her pocket" (pp. 112–13)—mark her as a daughter of the Puritans. It is appropriate that she does not share Mrs. Farrinder's practical aims of suffrage and temperance but instead is concerned with the history of women, which she casts in the Manichean terms of the Puritan divine. The Puritan viewed history as a long period of darkness, about to be ended by the intervention of God once again in human affairs and the final putting to rout of Satan. In Olive's view, only the names are changed: the history of mankind is the history of womankind; Satan is the male sex:

> The unhappiness of women! The voice of their silent suffering was always in her ears, the ocean of tears that they had shed from the beginning of time seemed to pour through her own eyes. Ages of oppression had rolled over them; uncounted millions had lived only to be tortured, to be crucified. They were her sisters, they were her own, and the day of their delivery had dawned. This was the only sacred cause; this was the great, the just revolution. It must triumph, it must sweep everything before it; it must exact from the other, the brutal, blood-stained, ravening race, the last particle of expiation! [pp. 37–38]

Verena represents the happier side of the New England heritage. That positive view of human experience that at its best gave rise to Transcendentalism and the abolitionist movement finds expression in her character, though by the 1870s this background has become as debased as Puritanism has in Olive. Verena's mother, the daughter of an abolitionist leader, is vague and flighty, devoid of both ideas and ideals—except that of seeing her daughter rise socially. Mr. Tarrant, veteran of the Cayuga Community and a mesmeric healer, has, as James hints, found ways acceptable to the New England philosophic tradition of dignifying and

indulging a licentious nature. And Verena's childhood was
an introduction to the numerous forms of self-improve-
ment and philanthropy that flourished in New England.
"She had been nursed in darkened rooms, and suckled in
the midst of manifestations; she had begun to 'attend lec-
tures'...when she was quite an infant, because her mother
had no one to leave her with at home. She had sat on the
knees of somnambulists, and had been passed from hand to
hand by trance-speakers; she was familiar with every kind of
'cure,' and had grown up among lady-editors of newspapers
advocating new religions, and people who disapproved of
the marriage-tie" (pp. 84–85). For someone with this background, the woman's movement is only another cause; any
other would have done as well. In this context, Verena's gift
of inspirational speaking and her talk of a world infused
with love seem an absurd reduction of Emerson's infusion
by the Spirit. Significantly, it is these two women, Verena
and Olive, who, with their lofty and abstract visions of the
future, command the public audience and the material
profit that Ransom can only dream of. While Verena's prettiness and her theatrical flare are a large part of her success,
she and Olive also succeed because they offer their public
what it wants to hear. Though they each envision different
futures, their New England backgrounds (as well as Northern victory in the war) have predisposed them to be for-
ward-looking and, in different ways, optimistic.

Having insisted on these regional differences, James can
use the conventional marriage of North and South only in
an ironic way. The two sides come together first in the Memorial Hall episode. Superficially, James's handling of this
event seems thoroughly conventional. Ransom visits Verena
at her parents' home in Cambridge for the first time. The
two of them walk through the Harvard campus and come
finally to Memorial Hall, an appropriate parallel to Adams's
Arlington Cemetery. Ransom studies the commemorative

tablets and pays the traditional homage to the foe: "he was capable of being a generous foeman, and he forgot, now, the whole question of sides and parties; the simple emotion of the old fighting-time came back to him, and the monument around him seemed an embodiment of that memory; it arched over friends as well as enemies, the victims of defeat as well as the sons of triumph" (p. 248). The mood of solemnity leads to a more intimate discussion with Verena than Ransom has ever had before, and the episode concludes with her tacit promise to keep the meeting a secret from Olive. A private relationship has been established that will ultimately lead to marriage.

In retrospect, we see that the union begun at Memorial Hall is only the most tenuous of alliances. North and South are simply too different to come together. On one side there is faith in social change, denial or sublimation of sexuality for an abstract goal, and resulting economic success; on the other, fear of change, aggressive perhaps compensatory sexuality, and economic failure. These are not grounds for reconciliation, and it is only because Verena's denial of sex has been made before her discovery of it (her red hair, after all, indicates a basically passionate nature, in spite of her immature figure) that the two sides are united at all. Verena responds finally to Ransom's sexuality: "She loved, she was in love—she felt it in every throb of her being. Instead of being constituted by nature for entertaining that sentiment in an exceptionally small degree (which had been the implication of her whole crusade, the warrant for her offer of old to Olive to renounce [marriage]), she was framed, apparently, to allow it the largest range, the highest intensity" (p. 396). Yet passion is not enough. The novel quite logically ends with James prophesying an unhappy future for her. The marriage of North and South is not the conventional symbolic affirmation of American union but a statement of the continuing discontents in American life. North and South are joined in an unhappy union, and man and woman remain at irreconcilable odds at the end of this romance. It is appropriate that the Memorial Hall episode, which is the beginning of the union of Verena and Ransom, is also the beginning of open warfare between Olive and Ransom who, as cousins, are symbolic of the divided Union.

In addition, the marriage at the end of the novel resolves the reformist issue in accord with James's convictions. Not only does Verena choose marriage instead of the woman's movement, but after all her talk of a better life for women, she accepts the one suitor of her several who will make her life a repetition of her mother's. Like her mother, she will come to feel that she has married beneath herself, for Verena, who delighted in the pretty things in Olive's Charles Street house and in Henry Burrage's Cambridge lodgings and who has it in her own power to earn a fortune, will doubtlessly chafe as the wife of a poor man—and Ransom, who proposes to Verena on the strength of one article accepted for publication, will doubtlessly remain a poor man. Like her mother, Verena will also come to feel a grudging and ambiguous respect for her husband: just as Mrs. Tarrant admires her husband for "an impudence so consummate that it had ended (in face of mortifications, exposures, failures, all the misery of a hand-to-mouth existence) by imposing itself on her as a kind of infallibility" (p. 74), so Verena will admire Ransom, who "would have despised himself if he had been capable of confessing to a woman that he couldn't make a living" (p. 205), and whose response to her questions about his difficulties getting published is a desire to silence her with a kiss. Verena's fate mocks the claims of a reform movement that has ignored human nature. While the marriage allows James an ironic variant of the Civil War romance, it also allows him a serious—if sobering—affirmation of the power of human sexuality.

In spite of its incidental humor, *The Bostonians* is a bitter and pessimistic novel. Its critical spirit does not lie simply in James's hostility to the woman's movement (it is significant that this is not accompanied by an endorsement of Ransom's patriarchal views) and his record of the conflicts in American life. Rather, the critical spirit of the novel lies in the awareness that underlies both these things, that is, in James's denial of that pervasive political myth of the eighties that the Civil War had not irreparably altered American life. Ransom thinks of the war as "an immense national *fiasco*" (p. 17); James, whose understanding is more mature, intimates throughout his novel that the war was a *tragedy* that had put men and women as well as North and South at odds and that it did not end at Appomattox.

In *The Bostonians* James had merged two popular genres to express this unpopular view of America. He had reworked both to emphasize the irreconcilable forces he saw at work around him with the result that both the texture and the conclusion of his novel could only bring the sort of discomfort that leads to a new awareness for the attentive reader. And he naively hoped for such readers. But the serialization attracted little attention, and there was no reason to expect the book to attract more. In addition, an insult added to injury, Osgood declared bankruptcy, leaving James unpaid for the serial.[19] James confessed to William, "I hoped much of it [*The Bostonians*], and shall be disappointed—having got no money for it, I hoped for a little glory."[20] When the book did come out, James's fears were confirmed. British reviewers virtually ignored it. The Boston-based *Literary World* noted the publication of the book by remarking, "Mr. Henry James's new novel, *The Bostonians*, we hear has proved an entire failure, and many booksellers are complaining that Mr. James's popularity has suddenly left him, much to their loss"[21]—a form of review that reminds us how much the mass reading public depended on previous sales in making its literary choices. More thoughtful American reviewers criticized the novel for its unpleasant characters and its slow-moving descriptive style. In doing this, they were focusing on features of the novel that serial publication had emphasized and that had undoubtedly put off many readers. A few reviewers saw that the long descriptions served to set up a contrast between North and South, but they could not or would not trace out the implications of that contrast. In their hesitation, they probably felt as did other readers who rejected the novel. Unlike James, an expatriate by the mid-eighties, even attentive readers could not afford to cast a cold critical eye on the myth of national unity. They had too much at stake.

THREE

The Princess Casamassima

At first glance, *The Princess Casamassima* seems to be as much an anomaly as *The Bostonians*. It has the distinction of being James's only full-length treatment of life among the poor. He was to deal with the subject in two later and shorter works, "Brooksmith" (1892) and "In the Cage" (1898), but the expansive concern with the subject in *The Princess* was sudden and unprecedented in his career. In a move which has, for the most part, foreclosed critical speculation on the origins of the novel, James claimed in his New York Edition preface that it was inspired by his own early experiences in London. As a newcomer to the city, he had roamed the streets, absorbing impressions and ideas. He had also been accepted by upper-class English society, something which few other Americans could boast of, though many dreamt of it. In conceiving of this novel, he had simply imagined what might have happened to himself instead of what actually did:

> I arrived so at the history of little Hyacinth Robinson—he sprang up for me out of the London pavement. To find his possible adventure interesting I had only to conceive his watching the same public show, the same innumerable appearances, I had watched myself, and of his watching very

much as I had watched; save indeed for one little difference.
This difference would be that so far as all the swarming facts
should speak of freedom and ease, knowledge and power,
money, opportunity and satiety, he should be able to revolve
round them but at the most respectful of distances and with
every door of approach shut in his face.[V, vi]

The Princess would record Hyacinth's (and James's vicarious)
desires in the face of such exclusion: the eagerness to be a
part of that rich, beautiful, and exclusive realm, and the
desire to destroy it. Like so many of James's works, it would
embody both his aristocratic and democratic sympathies.

There is no reason to question James's straightforward-
ness in the preface to *The Princess.* Hyacinth is treated so
indulgently in this novel that we cannot doubt James's claim
of partial identification with his protagonist. However, the
preface does not tell the whole story of the genesis of the
novel, for it does not explain what led James to break with
his past practice and write a novel dealing with working-
class life, and it does not explain how he accumulated and
organized material about a subject so foreign to him. James
had come to London to stay in 1876. Just as a recognition of
The Bostonians as a competitor in the mass market enables us
to understand why that novel took the form it did, so a
similar consideration of *The Princess* will help us to understand why, after nearly ten years, James wrote a novel
rooted in the memories of his early years in London but
cast in the guise of a story of working-class people.

In her autobiography, Beatrice Webb characterized the
eighties and nineties in England in a manner particularly
pertinent to *The Princess*: "There were...two controversies
raging in periodicals and books...on the one hand, the
meaning of the poverty of masses of men; and, on the
other, the practicability and desirability of political and industrial democracy as a set-off to, perhaps as a means of

redressing, the grievances of the majority of the people."[1] The meaning of poverty and the redressing of grievances are two of the central themes of James's novel. While James's periodical reading probably overlapped only slightly with Webb's, his friendships with other writers and with political figures, his club memberships, and his habit of reading newspapers acquainted him, as we know from his letters and his "London" essay, with the two controversies she mentions. When he decided to write a novel about working-class life, he was thus choosing to write a topical novel—despite its personal relevance.

James's method, when he began, was appropriate to his subject. In spite of his distaste for the French Naturalists' lack of discretion, we know he admired their seriousness and their enthusiasm for documentation. Following their lead, he did extensive research on various aspects of working-class life. In 1884, he wrote to Thomas Sergeant Perry, "I have been all morning at Millbank prison (horrible place) collecting notes for a fiction scene. You see I am quite the Naturalist. Look out for the same—a year hence."[2] In his notebook he recorded "Phrases, of the people" (*N*, p. 69) similar to those repeated in the Sun and Moon Café scene in the novel. And there must have been additional research trips and more notations—Oscar Cargill, for example, theorizes that the "London" essay was made up of material left over from the novel[3]—but no other records survive.

But James's memories and research were still not enough. When he actually began writing *The Princess*, he found himself floundering. He confided in his notebook: "I have never yet become engaged in a novel in which, after I had begun to write and send off my MS., the details had remained so vague" (*N*, p. 68). He felt that the major difficulty was that he was still writing *The Bostonians*, which was proving twice as long as originally anticipated.[4] He needed time, he said, to concentrate on *The Princess* and to allow his

subject matter to find an appropriate form. But having con-
tracted to produce both novels at once, he found that time
was not to be had. Cargill, after noting Daniel Lerner's discussion of parallels between *The Princess* and Turgenev's *Virgin Soil* (1877), suggests that James sought a way out of his
confusion with *The Princess* by borrowing Turgenev's basic
plot and adapting many of his characters. The result, he
concludes, is that *The Princess* is James's "most derivative
book."[5] Yet *Virgin Soil* cannot be as exclusive a source as
Cargill and Lerner suggest. Although James's plot and his
male characters Hyacinth Robinson and Paul Muniment
have close equivalents in Turgenev, his female characters are
quite different and his concern with familial relations and
urban life as conditioning factors in Hyacinth's life finds no
parallel in Turgenev's novel. James probably also looked to
English material for help. In the letter to William forecast-
ing the failure of *The Bostonians,* he noted his efforts to
make *The Princess* tighter and therefore more readable than
its predecessor, and added, "The *Princess* will, I trust, appear
more 'popular.'"[6] He could express this hope because *The
Princess* was similar in appearance to the English working-
class novel, one of the most popular genres of the eighties.[7]

The two writers in the genre whom James is most likely to
have read are George Gissing and Walter Besant. By the
time that James wrote *The Princess,* Gissing had written two
working-class novels—*Workers in the Dawn* (1880) and *The
Unclassed* (1884); he published a third (anonymously, however), *Demos* (1886), while James was in the midst of writing
and serializing *The Princess.* When James wrote about Gissing in 1897 ("London," *Harper's Weekly,* 31 July), he noted
that his admiration for the author dated from *New Grub
Street* (1891). His personal acquaintance with Gissing dated
from even later—1901. But James's enthusiastic discussion
of Gissing's portrayal of working-class life implies acquain-
tanceship with the earlier novels, and similarities between

those novels—especially *Workers in the Dawn* —and *The Princess* suggest that the acquaintance was made before *The Princess* was written. Gissing's novels made use of a popular genre but lacked popular appeal. Besant's novels, on the other hand, were best sellers. James was probably acquainted with his *All Sorts and Conditions of Men: An Impossible Story* (1882) when he took on Besant in "The Art of Fiction." It is unlikely that he would have taken public issue with an author whose recent and much talked about work was unknown to him, and Robert Louis Stevenson's subsequent answer to James ("A Humble Remonstrance") implies a mutual knowledge of the book. Besant's second working-class novel, *Children of Gibeon,* was serialized in *Longman's Magazine* in 1886 from January to December, while James was working on *The Princess.* Since "The Art of Fiction" had been published in *Longman's* and many of James's friends (Edmund Gosse, Howells, Violet Hunt, Justin McCarthy, Stevenson) were regularly published there, he may well have looked at the magazine while Besant's novel was appearing and while he was struggling with the details of his own book.

In addition to Gissing's and Besant's work, there are numerous other examples of the working-class novel. George Bernard Shaw, for example, tried his hand at it in *An Unsocial Socialist* (1884), an amusing but didactic book. Grant Allen, a sociologist and novelist who tried every popular fictional genre of the eighties and nineties from the feminist novel to the detective story, tried this one too with *Philistia* (1885). And Silas K. Hocking, a Methodist minister whom Arnold Bennett in 1901 described as "probably the most popular of living novelists,"[8] produced *Her Benny* (1879) and *Cricket: A Tale of Humble Life* (1880). The extraordinary range of authors testifies to just how popular the working-class novel was. Along with Gissing's and Besant's work, these books define the conventions of the genre and so allow us to reconstruct the context within which James wrote.

All of these working-class novels were written by middle-class authors for middle-class readers. Like *The Princess,* they were frequently the product of careful observation and research, and they show an awareness of the political interests and distinctive way of life of the urban working-class that was new in literature. But at the same time, the authors of these novels inevitably betray their middle-class bias by shying away from the implications of their discovery of working-class life. We see this clearly in their refusal to make political activity more than peripheral to the main story, for to do so would be to recognize the explosive potential of the exploited working class. When political ideas are entertained—as they are in the works of Besant, Shaw, and Allen, and in Gissing's *Demos*—socialism is the most acceptable scheme for the future because of its affinities with early Christianity, but a socialist society is foreseen as something that will come about only in the distant future.

The plots of these novels are equally evasive of the real problems of working-class life. There are two basic plots in the books noted above, both of which reaffirm England's class structure and at the same time insist that the gulf between classes need not be a source of discontent by claiming that the poor can be just like the rich. In both of Besant's novels, in Gissing's *Workers in the Dawn,* and in Allen's and Shaw's novels, members of the upper classes live among the workers and practice philanthropy with the ultimate aim of making the workers over in their own image. This plot receives its fullest and most maudlin exposition in Besant's novels, where a wealthy young heiress—in each book—lives among the poor under an assumed name. She teaches her companions to be neat and clean, establishes sewing cooperatives, cheers up the unhappy, and performs innumerable acts of charity—including building a recreation and cultural center for the entire East End in *All Sorts and Conditions,* a gesture that so captured the popular imagination as to provide the impetus for a real-life, subscription-supported People's Palace. At the end of each novel, the magnanimous heroine affirms her sympathy with the working class by marrying a man of working-class origin — one, however, who has been educated above his station.

The other common plot is used as a subplot by Besant, but it is central to all of Gissing's novels and to Hocking's. Here a working-class individual grows up and out of his own class by a combination of luck and initiative. This plot is most fully realized by Hocking; too many of Gissing's characters destroy themselves by following in the steps of their creator and making foolish marriages just when they are at the point of emerging into a better life. In both of Hocking's novels, a young man of intelligence and sensitivity is alone in the world. He succeeds in finding proper surrogate parents and in avoiding evil companions. In both novels he has the fortune to meet a girl who encourages and inspires him. Ultimately he prospers and, of course, marries the girl. While the descent-to-working-class-life plot might have been inspired by the fashion among the rich for visiting the slums to dole out bread and soup ("slumming"), the rise-from-poverty plot is of older origin. Dickens used and reused it — *Oliver Twist* and *Great Expectations* are obvious examples. It is inevitable that the plot should appear in the working-class novel, since no English urban novelist — including James in *The Princess* — could possibly write without some memory of Dickens's work. Furthermore, this particular plot, as Lionel Trilling has pointed out, is the mythical basis of innumerable fairy tales,[9] and it is not surprising that it should appear in a genre as evasive of real life as the late-nineteenth-century working-class novel.

As he had in *The Bostonians,* James works within and against popular conventions in *The Princess.* Again he brings two plots together — here the descent to working-class life and the rise from it. But instead of merging them as he had in *The Bostonians,* he plays them off against each other: as the Princess Casamassima, Christina Light, descends fur- ther and further into working-classs London, Hyacinth's experiences ally him increasingly with a realm of leisure time, money, and beauty. And then, James goes against conventional expectations and denies each character fulfill- ment: the Princess finds that she cannot penetrate the work- ing-class revolution as she would like, and Hyacinth cannot turn his back on his working-class origins and sympathies. I suggested that James's rejection of the dominant mood in American writing in the early and middle eighties lay be- hind his resistance to the reconciliatory design of the Civil War romance; a similar resistance to popular thinking is at work in his rejection of the meliorative patterns of the work- ing-class novel.

Implicit in novels like Besant's and Hocking's is an op- timistic view of human nature and the human situation. Both authors assume that the individual can know good and by conscious endeavor can modify his life in the direc- tion of that good. Both preach the traditional Protestant virtues of self-reliance, hard work, cleanliness, and honesty; both assure us through their plots that the practice of such virtues will bring material improvement and spiritual satis- faction to our lives. Such a view ignores the rapidly shifting class lines of the eighties and the unknown possibilities and problems posed for mankind by industrialism and urban- ism. The future is assumed to be just like the past and is therefore reckoned comprehensible and predictable. For James, in the mid-eighties, such a simplistic view of life was impossible. As *The Princess* indicates, he saw clearly the ever- widening gulf between the rich and poor and knew some- thing about the growing political and labor movements of the period. But what he had to offer instead of optimism was an indistinct vision of man's condition and future, col- ored by both fear and uncertainty.

Contemporary reviews usually described *The Princess* as a novel about socialism, but comparison of James's novel with others cited in the reviews[10] and with those mentioned here shows this description to be the result of carelessness or preconception. James chose to deal with anarchism, not socialism, in *The Princess,* a deliberate choice that is an important indication of the vision behind the novel. He may have been inspired by the anarchists of *Virgin Soil* or, as W. H. Tilley has argued, by the frequent discussions of anarchism in the *London Times,*[11] but he must also have been aware that insofar as the contemporary English working-class novel was political, it embraced socialism. Socialism, as it is discussed in Besant, Shaw, and Allen, threatened to undo the present social order, but the change would come in the future and would bring with it an order that was rational and just. Anarchism, as James understood it, offered only imminent destruction. He depicts the anarchist movement vaguely and melodramatically. Irving Howe has praised James's understanding of the political personality, but, as Howe also notes, James communicates little understanding of either the philosophy or actual operation of the movement. Tilley and Trilling have both tried to justify James's vagueness—Tilley by claiming that the *Times* stories James read were vague and Trilling by arguing that the anarchist movement in fact lacked a tight structure.[12] But these justifications are finally irrelevant. By depicting the anarchist movement as vaguely as he has, James indicates that his interest is in what the revolutionary movement symbolizes to his characters and to himself rather than in how it actually functions.

In *The Princess,* the anarchist movement, with its vague politics and unspecified program for the future, expresses both the unarticulated rage of an exploited working class and the fears of an author who, as we know from his letters, saw widespread discontent around him and looked apprehensively to the future. When Hyacinth has fully committed himself to working with the anarchists, he is permitted to know "the holy of holies" (VI, 48), a truth that changes his understanding of the nature of reality.[13] He tells the Princess what he now knows, speaking in metaphoric terms because, as he says, "It's beyond anything I can say" (VI, 49). His heightened language conveys the impact of his new vision in a way that literal facts alone could not:

> Nothing of it appears above the surface; but there's an immense underworld peopled with a thousand forms of revolutionary passion and devotion.... And on top of it all society lives! People go and come, and buy and sell, and drink and dance, and make money and make love, and seem to know nothing and suspect nothing and think of nothing; and iniquities flourish, and the misery of half the world is prated about as a "necessary evil," and generations rot away and starve in the midst of it, and day follows day, and everything is for the best in the best of possible worlds. All that's one half of it; the other half is that everything's doomed! In silence, in darkness, but under the feet of each one of us, the revolution lives and works. It's a wonderful, immeasurable trap, on the lid of which society performs its antics.... The invisible impalpable wires are everywhere, passing through everything, attaching themselves to objects in which one would never think of looking for them. [VI, 49]

In a frenzied world on the brink of dissolution, the meliorative gestures of those who descend to working-class life and the social aspirations of those who rise from it are pointless: "everything's doomed."

The forebodings James shares with Hyacinth dictate his handling of his main characters. The Princess most obviously deviates in both her motivations and fate from her fictional peers. Besant's Angela Messenger (*All Sorts and Conditions*) owns a brewery that employs most of London's

East End and owns most of the surrounding property. Since her family originated in the East End, and since a large part of the area is now dependent on her, she feels a moral obligation to learn about lower-class life and to do what she can to help the people who work for her. Valentine Eldridge (*Children of Gibeon*) has been raised in society with Violet, formerly Polly Monument,[14] daughter of a washerwoman and petty thief, whom her mother has adopted. Neither girl knows which of them is the true daughter and heiress of Sir Lancelot Eldridge. Before their identities are revealed, Valentine goes to live with Polly's sister and her friends, and after she learns that she is the heiress, decides to remain with the poor girls because she loves them and knows she can help them. Gissing's philanthropic heroine is less sentimentally drawn. Helen Norman (*Workers in the Dawn*) decides, after a course of philosophic study, that one's responsibility on earth is to one's brothers and that the rich have a special responsibility to the poor. Like Besant's heroines, she is rich enough to embark on a program of philanthropic work—but Gissing is realistic enough to have her discover that running a school for working girls is the only thing she can do effectively; prodigal charity of the type practiced by Besant's heroines does not really alter the conditions of the poor. These characters are traditional Victorian heroines, idealized women, motivated by a sense of duty, acting in a predictable world in which individual effort counts. They meet traditional fates: Besant's heroines marry happily; Gissing's heroine—representing a darker tradition—dies of consumption when she learns that the man she loves cannot marry her.

In his preface to the New York Edition of *The Princess*, James noted that his heroine, Christina Light, had haunted him since her creation in *Roderick Hudson* (1875). A more immediate impulse, forgotten, suppressed, or perhaps never consciously acknowledged, may also lie behind

Christina's resurrection in *The Princess*. At the end of 1883,
F. Marion Crawford published *To Leeward*. It is the story of a
half-Russian, half-English girl who amuses herself by reading and discussing modern philosophies. She marries a dull
but good Italian marchese, is immediately bored, and soon
begins seeing a conceited, cold-hearted Englishman. She
eventually runs away with him; her husband follows and,
insane with anger, shoots at his rival but kills his wife instead. The book was an immediate popular success, and its
reception prompted James to write to Howells in despair
and anger, "What you tell me of the success of Crawford's
last novel sickens & almost paralyses me.... I would rather
have produced the basest experiment in the 'naturalism'
that is being practiced here than such a piece of sixpenny
humbug. Work so shamelessly bad seems to me to dishon-
our the novelist's art to a degree that is absolutely not to be
forgiven."[15] In returning to his own discontented heroine
and continuing her story along the lines laid out by
Crawford, James was either consciously trying to improve
on *To Leeward* or he was unconsciously recalling and imitating a pattern that had proved successful with the public.
Either response testifies to his grasp of popular conventions
and his desire to appeal to the mass market in *The Princess*.
His comment on English naturalism, of which the working-
class novel is representative, is a further reminder to us of
his knowledge of contemporary tastes.

By resurrecting Christina and casting her in the role of
the "slumming" upper-class lady, James was giving his novel
a heroine whose background and therefore motives were
radically different from that of her fictional counterparts.
While Christina's fictional peers are upper-class English
ladies, she has no fixed social station. She is half American,
half Italian, haphazardly educated, more traveled than settled, and a representative of upper-class life only because of
her marriage to a wealthy prince. It is a background that

disposes her to unconventional and unconstrained behavior. She is not motivated by any sort of idealism; as Hyacinth astutely recognizes, "personal passion had counted for so much in the formation of her views" (V, 295). Her interest in revolution dates from a quarrel with her husband and is colored by resentment of him for trying to control her and by resentment of the titled and moneyed class he represents. Her interest in the poor is sporadic and fitful, an amusing game or a role to be adopted at will. But her hatred of the rich is a burning passion. She tells Hyacinth that after a year and a half in England, she has come to know the upper classes: "It's the old régime again, the rottenness and extravagance, bristling with every iniquity and every abuse, over which the French Revolution passed like a whirlwind; or perhaps even more a reproduction of the Roman world in its decadence, gouty, apoplectic, depraved, gorged and clogged with wealth and spoils, selfishness and scepticism, and waiting for the onset of the barbarians" (V, 23). James himself was later to use this same formulation in a letter to describe England's condition—without the breathy abundance of adjectives and with an added expression of sympathy for the poor.[16] The Princess, however, has little room for sympathy; what she wants is assurance that the revolution is imminent, that the class she hates will be destroyed.

The egotism that refers the problem of social change to her need for vengeance prevents the Princess from ultimately gaining the knowledge she seeks. When she first meets Hyacinth, she tells him, "I wanted to know something, to learn something, to ascertain what really is going on; and for a woman everything of that sort's so difficult" (V, 215). In seeking a man to help her, she is guided not only by her political interests but also by her resentment of her husband. She is always looking for a man who is his opposite, whose strength of character she will be compelled to respect, whose masculinity she will find seductive. It is logical that she should look at the end of the social scale opposite her husband's. She recalls the anarchist leader Hoffendahl as such a man and recognizes Paul Muniment as another. Her betrayal of Hyacinth for Muniment is inevitable. But in choosing Muniment over Hyacinth, she defeats her own aim. While he can offer her the domination she wants, he cannot offer her the knowledge. His liaison with the Princess discredits him in the anarchist movement, and directions given to Hyacinth to commit murder on behalf of the revolutionaries—proof positive that the revolution is alive and well—are not entrusted to Muniment. In the end it is Hyacinth who, though he lacks the force of character and the virility that the Princess craves, possesses the knowledge. The Princess's failure is not an indication of the futility of the kind of idealism dramatized in the conventional descent-to-the-slums story; the ineffectual Lady Aurora serves that function for James. Rather, the Princess's fate is an illustration of the Jamesian rule that true insight comes only to the sensitive who can put aside the claims of self. Her story illuminates Hyacinth's.

In contrast to the Princess, whom we find a recognizable type, Hyacinth strikes many modern readers as too precious to be anything but singular and so indulgently created as to suggest not merely semi-identification with his creator but self-pitying autobiography.[17] But in fact, comparison of Hyacinth with other working-class heroes shows him to be more conventional in character than the Princess— although his fate is as unconventional as hers. Hyacinth's story is a variant on the rise-from-poverty story, complete with surrogate parents (Miss Pynsent, Mr. Vetch, the Poupins) and lovely ladies who are ambiguously both sisters and sweethearts (Millicent Henning and the Princess) to help him. His character effectively complicates his story, for he is as sensitive to the sufferings of the poor as he is attracted to the pleasures of the rich. With a bow to French Naturalism and to the less theoretical naturalism of the English working-class novel,[18] James accounts for Hyacinth in terms of blood and environment. His mother was a seamstress, the daughter of a French republican and the murderer of his presumed father, an English peer. He is the unhappy embodiment of these two elements: "There was no peace for him between the two currents that flowed in his nature, the blood of his passionate plebeian mother and that of his long-descended supercivilised sire. They continued to toss him from one side to the other; they arrayed him in intolerable defiances and revenges against himself" (VI, 264). It is not only external obstacles that such a character must surmount in order to rise.

Lerner and Cargill see a similarity between Hyacinth and Turgenev's Nezhdanov (in *Virgin Soil*), the illegitimate son of a nobleman and a commoner, a man with poetical gifts and anarchist sympathies but of too passive a nature to act. But the divided character is also a convention of the English working-class novel. The working-class protagonist closest to Hyacinth—and he is closer than Nezhdanov—is Gissing's tormented Arthur Golding in *Workers in the Dawn*. Golding is orphaned as a child, raised by a poor printer in London whose close friends are political radicals, and gifted with extraordinary artistic talent. His life appears to be an unresolvable struggle: "As he grew older he felt within himself the stirrings of a double life, the one, due to his natural gifts, comprehending all the instincts, the hopes, the ambitions of the artist; the other, originating in the outward circumstances of his childhood...which urged him on to the labours of the philanthropist, showing him in the terribly distinct reflex of his own imagination the ever-multiplying miseries of the poor amongst whom he lived.... These two distinct impulses seemed to grow within Arthur Golding's mind with equal force and rigidity...."[19] Besant's male protagonists also struggle. In both *All Sorts and Conditions* and *Children of Gibeon,* a man of working-class origin who has been raised and educated by a wealthy benefactor feels as an adult that he must choose between commitment to his adoptive social class and work on behalf of his original class. While the terms of the conflict are slightly different for James, Gissing, and Besant, the notion of competing loyalties which complicate the sought-for rise from the slums is central to all three.

Gissing's and Besant's novels work toward a reconciliation of conflict. In James's book, as in his previous one, reconciliation is impossible, for once again, James cannot accept the optimistic fantasies that lay behind popular fiction. Hyacinth's childhood and adult experience intensify the conflict within him. As a child he is raised in poverty by Miss Pynsent and taken to visit his dying mother in prison; but Miss Pynsent also fills his head with romantic nonsense about his noble connections and encourages his instinctive gentlemanly ways. As an adult, he finds himself torn between two daydreams:

> When he himself was not letting his imagination wander among the haunts of the aristocracy and stretching it in the shadow of an ancestral beech to read the last number of the *Revue des Deux Mondes* he was occupied with contemplations of a very different kind; he was absorbed in the struggles and sufferings of the millions whose life flowed in the same current as his and who, though they constantly excited his disgust and made him shrink and turn away, had the power to chain his sympathy, to raise it to passion, to convince him for the time at least that real success in the world would be to do something with them and for them. [V, 163]

Subsequent events give substance to the daydreams. His experience of working-class life, his friendship with Muni-

ment, and his involvement with the anarchists whet his desire to serve the poor to the point where he agrees to
commit a political murder. At the same time, his friendship
with the Princess, his visit to Medley, her country house (his
dream come true, down to the detail of the *Revue*), and his
trip to the Continent after Miss Pynsent's death, push him
further and further away from his pledge to the anarchists.
He cannot resolve his conflict and instead comes to see it in
increasingly impersonal terms. On the Continent he discovers, as he writes to the Princess, that "The monuments
and treasures of art, the great palaces and properties, the
conquests of learning and taste, the general fabric of civil-
isation as we know it," are precious even though they have
cost "all the despotisms, the cruelties, the exclusions, the
monopolies and the rapacities of the past" (VI, 145). But on
returning home, he is overwhelmed by the immense
amount of privation and suffering he sees among London's
working people, and he feels that things must change:
"What was most in Hyacinth's mind was the idea, of which
every pulsation of the general life of his time was a syllable,
that the flood of democracy was rising over the world; that
it would sweep all the traditions of the past before it" (VI,
262). Having glimpsed the revolution stirring beneath the
surface of society, Hyacinth ultimately cannot doubt its reality, though he can wish it were not so.

When Hyacinth finally receives orders to kill a nobleman,
he chooses, instead, to kill himself. Had he received his
orders shortly after his return from the Continent, his
death, as Trilling eloquently argues, would testify to his
total awareness of the human plight.[20] But James's novel
continues past this point. When Hyacinth's orders do come,
he finds that his friends have drifted from him—Muniment
has abandoned him to a cause he knows Hyacinth now only
reluctantly accepts; Milly and Captain Sholto have become
lovers, as have the Princess and Muniment—and that his

surrogate parents, though sensing his difficulties, cannot understand him enough to intervene effectively. Hyacinth thinks of his behavior in the end, not in political or social terms but in personal terms. Having been betrayed by his "parents" and friends, he recognizes now that if he does kill the nobleman, that too will be an act of betrayal—and one against the only parent whose relationship to himself he is sure is genuine: "the idea of the personal stain [of murder] made him horribly sick; it seemed by itself to make service impossible. It passed before him, or rather it stayed, like a blow dealt back at his mother, already so hideously disfigured; to suffer it to start out in the life of her son was in a manner to place her own forgotten redeemed pollution again in the eye of the world" (VI, 419).[21] His final choice of suicide over murder is both an act of integrity which dissociates him from the people whom he earlier identified with— he will not be a betrayer, even though they are—and an act of despair, for he is totally abandoned by the end of the novel.

James's narrowing of his subject from the political and social to the personal gives the last part of *The Princess* a rather disjointed quality. The relationship between the political and personal issues is allusive at best.[22] Further, the shift diminishes Hyacinth; he is no longer the tormented social observer but instead the hapless, betrayed child. Still, if we consider the conventions within which James was working, the shift to the personal does make sense. The rise-from-poverty story—unlike *Virgin Soil*—always treats the hero in familial terms. The surrogate parents and inspiring ladies are an essential part of these stories and typically aid the hero in resolving his situation in a satisfactory manner. Hocking's heroes are inspired to work hard, be honest, and thereby improve their social standing; Besant's heroes are taught to work for the amelioration of the poor; one of the protagonists of Gissing's *The Unclassed* is adopted and given a decent job which will allow him time to write and money to marry on; Arthur Golding in *Workers in the Dawn,* the Gissing character most like Hyacinth, is encouraged to maintain a humane concern for the lower classes while devoting himself primarily to art—but he ultimately destroys himself by a foolish marriage. The conclusion to *The Princess,* however, is a denial of the usual sentimental and optimistic resolution of popular fiction. Hyacinth cannot resolve his conflicts, and those around him abandon rather than aid him. If, as I am suggesting, the betrayals Hyacinth suffers are offered in contrast to the usual pattern of human behavior in popular fiction, we can understand the dissolution of personal relationships in this novel as emblematic of a world in which all traditional order is felt to be on the verge of destruction. It is an appropriate, though not fully adequate, sign of a world in which "everything's doomed."

Because *The Princess* embodies James's rejection of the facile optimism of the working-class novel, the book must claim our serious attention in a way that its counterparts cannot. By rejecting the self-conscious hopefulness of the period and therefore the plot patterns that enshrined such a perspective, James asks us to confront a profoundly dark view of the world. And yet the book is disappointing. Although James was able to rework major conventions of the working-class novel to his advantage, he was not able to escape a significant limitation of the genre. By shying away from an examination of the real discontents of working-class life, the working-class novel gave practitioners of the form no way of relating character and historical circumstance. Characters were typically rather idealized figures appropriate to the escapist plots but not to actual fact. James's limited knowledge of the English political scene, his long-standing concern with character, and the pressure under which he wrote his novel all made it easy for him to adopt this typical disjunction between character and context.[23]

Neither the Princess nor Hyacinth is clearly a product of the eighties and so lacks the representative quality that dignifies and enlarges characters like Isabel Archer and Christopher Newman—or Olive Chancellor and Basil Ransom. The knowledge that the Princess seeks and with which Hyacinth is both blessed and burdened stands as an implicit criticism of the inadequacy of the popular working-class novel. But because the two characters do not represent something more than themselves, their fates tell us little about the social and political situation of the eighties. We see instead an egotist who fails in her quest and a sensitive innocent who is immobilized by what he learns and by what he suffers at the hands of friends. *The Princess,* with its dense, detailed surface seems, at first glance, to be one of those books that is a richly informative account of its time; in the end, it has little specific to tell us.

Even while James was working on *The Princess,* another genre was emerging—one that would tell us more about the lives of working people and the relevance of social and political action to them than the working-class novel could. This was the novel that depicted the conflict of labor and capital. But it was not a genre that James could experiment with. The numerous strikes of the late eighties and nineties may have educated James as they educated much of the public, but they came too late for his novel. Furthermore, since response to a topical issue was not only response to the issue itself for James but also to popular thinking in the form of popular fiction, he needed the impetus of literary precedent to write—and this was missing. There were few examples of the labor-versus-capital novel in the eighties and never many English examples at all, though the genre later became an important American form. We know of only one such novel that James read before he wrote *The Princess.* This was a timid and conservative book by his friend John Hay, *The Breadwinners* (serialized anonymously in the *Century*, August 1883 to January 1884). James was not particularly enthusiastic about it; he guessed the work was Hay's and recommended it to his sister with slightly humorous but real reservations: "It has a great deal of crude force & is a guide (lately) fait [*sic*] de mieux in the American novel, after Howells & me."[24] Hay's novel, with its American setting and unfamiliar treatment of politics, could not serve as a model for James. Indeed James could have written his own novel only as he did. And while he failed to tell us very much about working-class life and its relationship to political activity, he at least succeeded in suggesting that the life of his time was more uncertain than many of his contemporaries thought and in denying the sentimentalities with which they diverted themselves and their audiences.

FOUR

The Tragic Muse

While James was working on *The Tragic Muse,* he contemplated changes in his professional life. In July 1888, when he began the book, he wrote to Stevenson that this was to be his last long novel.[1] This seems to have been a decision prompted in large part by weariness and frustration: the novel, as James was producing it in the eighties, took too long to write and attracted too little popular attention, and he rightly sensed that *The Tragic Muse* was going to be a repeat performance.[2] In the midst of his work on the book, another possibility presented itself when Edmund Compton offered to back a dramatic production of *The American.* It is not surprising therefore that critics have looked at *The Tragic Muse,* a novel about artists and the demands of their work, as an apologia with special relevance to the impending changes in James's career. Lyall Powers, for example, speaks of the book as a metaphoric farewell to the novel and a somewhat hesitant welcome to the theater; Donald David Stone sees in it a defense of the artist's absolute commitment to his art whatever its form; and Leon Edel finds it a reluctant acknowledgment of the loneliness that commitment to high art entails.[3] James's professional worries undoubtedly influenced his actual writing, and it is fair to see some degree of personal meaning in the book. But the book's genesis antedated James's extreme difficulties in the marketplace and his consequently contemplated professional changes. Like *The Bostonians* and *The Princess Casamassima, The Tragic Muse* —as contemporary reviewers recognized[4]—was conceived and developed in response to topical issues, in this case the theater, aestheticism, and the changing relations between the sexes.

Although James could recall himself working on *The Tragic Muse* in London and Paris, he claimed in the New York Edition preface "a certain vagueness of remembrance in respect to the origin and growth" of the novel and insisted, "I can but look on the present fiction as a poor fatherless and motherless, a sort of unregistered and unacknowledged birth" (VII, v). This confession was then followed by an account of the technical difficulties encountered in writing the book, an account which, in fact, describes the way the novel evolved. According to James here, he began with the parallel stories of Nick Dormer, who was to give up politics for art, and Peter Sherringham, who was to refuse a like sacrifice; Miriam Rooth, an actress who is the Tragic Muse of the title, then struck him as supplying the keystone that would bind the two stories (VII, vii– xiv). Yet the parallel developed in the novel itself is that of Nick and Miriam, two artists who must find some way of resisting the art-threatening claims of "the world," to use James's terminology (VII, v). We begin to suspect that the evolution James traces here is a fabrication, following as it does on his insistence on "vagueness of remembrance" and being out of accord with the book itself—a suspicion strengthened by James's misestimation of Miriam: he claims she would have been willing to "chuck" her career for Nick for "the glory... of their common infatuation with 'art'" (VII, xviii), thereby denying her the central, serious role she has in the book.

In all likelihood, James had not completely forgotten the origin of his novel, and his preface was indeed designed to obscure rather than to enlighten. In December 1878, James reviewed *Macleod of Dare* for the *Nation*; its author was William Black, a prolific writer of popular but trivial romances. *Macleod of Dare* is the story of a Scottish laird who falls in love with Gertrude White, an English actress; he proposes to her, she accepts and agrees to leave the stage for him; but the attractions of London life and promise of fame are too strong, and she breaks the engagement; Macleod, in whom the barbaric traditions of his ancestors still live, abducts Gerty and sails for Scotland with her; a storm springs up and the two are drowned. Not surprisingly James found much to criticize in the novel, but for him Black's greatest failure was his handling of the actress:

> Gertrude White is not the least the study of an actress, nor indeed, as it seems to us, the study of anything at all. The author had an admirable chance; nothing could have been more dramatic than to bring out the contrast between the artistic temperament, the histrionic genius and Bohemian stamp of the *femme de théâtre,* and the literal mind and purely moral development of her stalwart Highland lover. But the contrast has been missed; Gertrude White, in so far as she has any identity, is almost as much a Puritan and a precisian as her lover; she is nothing of a Bohemian, and we doubt very much whether she was anything of an actress. It was a very gratuitous stroke on Mr. Black's part to represent her as one.[5]

In referring to Black's actress as a Puritan, James was undoubtedly recalling her occasional agreement with Macleod's criticism of the protean character of the actress: "What must the end of it be?—that you play with emotions and beliefs until you have no faith in any one—none left for yourself—it is only the material of your art."[6] We see in James's interest in the character of the actress and in the difficulties she might encounter with a conventional suitor the germ of his own novel. Far from being added as a keystone, James's actress was probably his cornerstone.

It is unlikely that James had forgotten Black's book by the time he came to write his own—Peter criticizes Miriam in much the same terms that Macleod does Gerty, and a number of smaller details also suggest James's recollection of the book—though he may have forgotten it by the time he wrote the preface. But *Macleod of Dare* was not his only source; a second source was more memorably inscribed. In June of 1884, James copied into his notebook an idea that Mrs. Humphry Ward had mentioned. Again we see his interest in the character of the actress:

> A young actress is an object of much attention and a great deal of criticism from a man who loves the stage...and finally, though she doesn't satisfy him at all, artistically, [he] loves the girl herself. He thinks something may be made of her, though he doesn't quite see what: he works over her, gives her ideas, etc. Finally (she is slow in developing, though full of ambition), she takes one, and begins to mount, to become a celebrity. She goes beyond him, she leaves him looking after her and wondering.... The interest, I say, would be as a study of a certain particular *nature d'actrice*.... The strong nature, the personal quality, vanity, etc. of the girl: her artistic being, so vivid, yet so purely instinctive. Ignorant, illiterate, Rachel. [*N*, pp. 63–64]

It is not clear whether James understood at this point that Mrs. Ward was writing the story herself, but by the end of the year her book *Miss Bretherton* appeared. Mrs. Ward had followed the plot James recorded with one important difference: her heroine, Isabel Bretherton, accepts a proposal of marriage at the height of her career and, so the novel implies, will abandon that career. Mrs. Ward's portrayal of the actress disturbed James enough for him to speak and to write to her about it. He complained that she had not adequately depicted the ambition, the egotism that enable an actress to succeed and that the actress who succeeded in consequence of those qualities would not act as Isabel does at the end of the novel. Perhaps Mrs. Ward's failure recalled Black's: "You have endeavoured to make us feel her 'respectability' at the same time as her talent, her artistic nature," he wrote to Mrs. Ward, "but in taking care to preserve the former, you have rather sacrificed the latter."[7] Nevertheless, Mrs. Ward's book was a popular success, and—notwithstanding James's complaints that the behavior of the actress was not convincing—Isabel Bretherton was oddly corroborated in the career of the actress Mary Anderson.[8]

In writing his New York Edition prefaces, James apparently looked back at his notebooks to recover lost "germs." In one preface he remarked on the mystery attending the birth of any story and observed, "One's notes, as all writers remember, sometimes explicitly mention, sometimes indirectly reveal, and sometimes wholly dissimulate, such clues and such obligations. The search for these last indeed, through faded or pencilled pages, is perhaps one of the sweetest of our more pensive pleasures" (XVII, xxi). He must have seen his notes for *The Tragic Muse*. In addition, James had met Mary Anderson and was therefore likely to remember his conferences with Mrs. Ward about the character of the actress even without the help of his notebooks. Why then did he profess "vagueness of remembrance" and discuss his novel so as to obscure the fact that the examination of the character of the actress was such a strong provocation for him? In part, James's silence was probably a tactful gesture, motivated by a wish not to provoke comparisons with the work of a friend. In part, perhaps, it reflects a desire to stress what was original in his own work. But above all, I believe James's silence is a response to the popular failure of his book. He remarked in his preface, "The influence of 'The Tragic Muse' was...exactly other than what I had all earnestly (if of course privately enough) invoked for it, and I remember well the particular chill, at least, of the sense of my having launched it in a great grey void from which no echo or message whatever would come back" (VII, vi). To add to this confession of failure that *The Tragic Muse* had attempted improvement on two popular novels would simply have been too painful. So James spoke as the Master he had become by the time of the New York Edition: the fabrication he presented was a convenient way of discussing the technical difficulties he encountered in writing the novel.

In spite of James's silence, one modern critic has named *Macleod of Dare* as a source for *The Tragic Muse* and several have named *Miss Bretherton*.[9] The contrasting characters of the actress and her suitor seem to have been suggested by Black's book, while the plot of the Miriam-Peter story seems to be derived from Mrs. Ward's. Both books contributed to James's minor characters, but Mrs. Ward's seems to have been the more influential. Mrs. Ward also raised a number of contemporary issues pertaining to the stage: the lack of discrimination among English theatergoers and the English preoccupation with the respectability of the actress provoked her criticism; the rigorous training the French stage demanded evoked praise. As we know from James's essays on the theater these were also issues of genuine interest to him. In addition, their inclusion gave *Miss Bretherton* a topical appeal that *Macleod of Dare* lacked. It is probably for this reason that *Miss Bretherton* inspired James in a way that *Macleod of Dare* had not. When he wrote his own story of an actress, he not only took over Mrs. Ward's plot and characters but also examined the same theatrical issues she had and seconded her opinions.

Consideration of theatrical questions added depth to James's novel (as it had to Mrs. Ward's), and it also reflected his (and her) involvement in the ongoing public discussion

of one of the major aesthetic concerns of the day. D. J.
Gordon and John Stokes survey the extensive discussion of
theater-related issues in the eighties and conclude:

> *The Tragic Muse* is "topical", as *The Bostonians* and *The Prin-*
> *cess Casamassima* are "topical", but is more precisely and ob-
> viously so than either (for good, or evil) in the way it relates
> to moment and debate. It can also be read as an attempt by
> James to "broaden his scope" and extend his audience....
> The closer topical relations of *The Tragic Muse* involved in
> fact a closer restriction of audience. The public world that
> *The Tragic Muse* comes from and points to is the world of
> "serious" papers, reviews and quarterlies. It was, indeed, a
> serious and important world, and definable because it was
> small and unified through class, culture, function.[10]

In other words, the particular topicality of *The Tragic Muse*
could have been expected to win it a small but select audience, a new audience for James and therefore an extension of his readership. If James was in fact seeking such an
audience with this novel, the book represents his first acknowledgment of his status as a minority writer. I think
James may have been moving in this direction without
being fully aware of the fact. But at the same time, the
popularity of *Miss Bretherton* must have suggested to him
that he could appeal to a mass audience even while investi-
gating issues of special interest to a few.

Mrs. Ward succeeded with the public because she had a
simple and eternally popular story to tell; her theatrical
concerns were secondary to her. Isabel Bretherton is cast in
the mold of the typical Victorian heroine: she has great
personal charm, delicate health, and a spotless personal
reputation which she jealously guards. She is completely
unformed as an actress at the beginning of the novel, for
she has had neither professional training nor worldly expe-

rience to call on in its stead—and thus possesses the innocence of the proper Victorian lady in spite of her
profession. An admirer, a rather retiring man of letters
named Eustace Kendal, tells her what qualities her art is
lacking and introduces her to his sister and brother-in-law.
The brother-in-law in turn educates the actress, teaching
her the traditions and skills she needs. Isabel is a most
responsive pupil: she is described as possessing "a nature on
which nothing is lost"[11] (Mrs. Ward's bow to James or a
common phrase?), and at the end of the novel, she is able to
return to the London stage for a triumphant second season.
When Kendal sees how much her acting has improved, how
little she needs him, he hesitates to ask her to marry him. At
the urging of his sister, fortuitously dying so her wishes
carry special weight, he proposes—and Isabel, dependent
and compliant as many Victorian heroines before her, con-
veniently and symbolically weakened by a recent illness, accepts him.

In view of such sentimentality, James's objections to Isabel Bretherton do seem justified. In telling his story,
James's interest in "a certain particular *nature d'actrice*"
would take him in a radically different direction—as would
his long-standing interest in the difficulties between the
sexes. Both *The Bostonians* and *The Princess* dramatize
failures of communication between men and women. In a
short dialogue called "An Animated Conversation" that
James published while *The Tragic Muse* was running, one of
the characters speaks of "The essential, latent antagonism of
the sexes—the armed opposed array of men and women,
founded on irreconcilable interests." This is not simply mis-
ogyny, but a perception that the conflict is "the huge 'issue'
of the future," erupting out of a change in contemporary
social arrangements; "Hitherto we have judged these interests reconcilable, and even practically identical. But all that
is changing because women are changing...."[12] For James a

story about an actress necessarily meant yet another dramatization of the war between men and women, because the
actress is, almost by definition, an egotist. James's conviction that the hostility between the sexes was of particular
interest to contemporary readers is, as I will indicate, ampli-
fied in the novel itself and may have provided some of the
ground for James's hopes for his novel in the mass market.

Miriam Rooth is not only an embodiment of James's idea
of the actress but also is a response to both Isabel Bretherton and Gertrude White. She is another one of James's anti-
Victorian heroines. Like the Princess Casamassima, she is
an outsider: in this case, the daughter of a Jewish father and
an English mother who claims descent from the "Neville-
Nugent[s] of Castle Nugent" (VII, 63). Isabel was only
mildly exotic by comparison—Scots and Venetian—and entirely acceptable to society. There is nothing ladylike about
Miriam: she has neither prettiness, nor charm, nor manners
but possesses both vitality and self-assurance with none of
Gerty's petty self-absorption. Given her hand-to-mouth existence and her mother's social incompetence, we are surprised to learn that Miriam has led a blameless life—and we
cannot help but feel that a Victorian timidity in dealing with
sex is at work here. But James handles the issue of Miriam's
morality gracefully. Mrs. Ward let Kendal voice her own
distaste for the actress's excessive prudery, and at the same
time avoided offending her audience by allowing Isabel to
retain her moral straitness. Though Miriam is no libertine,
the suggestion of prudery never arises either. Miriam's respectability stems partly from her good-natured yielding to
her mother who wants to see her marry well, and more
important, from her utter indifference to anything irrelevant to her acting. For she is above all an actress. Like
Isabel, she is untaught but quick to learn; like Gerty, she has
the gift of plasticity without which training can do nothing.
And she is tenacious and devoted: while Gerty hesitates to

leave the stage because she will miss the adulation that goes with it, Miriam is devoted to her art itself—to the challenge of a difficult role, the privilege of moving people, and the pure sensuous pleasure of acting.

Peter is as cautious a suitor as Kendal but less willing to consider the possibility that the woman he loves does not need him. He is a career diplomat with a strong sense of self-worth and a conviction that "Ambition, in the career, was probably consistent with marrying—but only with opening one's eyes very wide to do it" (VII, 316). Oddly enough for one who feels this way, he is not bothered by the stigma Miriam's background or profession might place on a man in government service. It is her devotion to her work that scares him at the same time that it attracts him. So he resists his feelings for her at first, telling himself that one cannot love an actress because one does not know what one is loving. Then he comes closer to admitting his feelings through several joking proposals of marriage. And at last, when he is ready to leave England, to incarcerate himself at his own request in a small, "shaky" (VIII, 223) Central American republic where he might forget his passion, he risks the consequences of an open confession of feeling: he asks her to give up her career, to devote herself to him instead, to become his wife.

Miriam at once detects the contradiction in his thinking: "You admire me as an artist and therefore you wish to put me into a box in which the artist will breathe her last. Ah, be reasonable; you must let her live!" Peter's answer is similar to Ransom's response to Verena in *The Bostonians* when she too asked what would become of her talent should she marry. He speaks patronizingly, reducing her artistic nature to a superior kind of social talent: "Don't talk about my putting you in a box, for, dearest child, I'm taking you out of one.... The artist is irrepressible, eternal; she'll be in everything you are and in everything you do, and you'll go

about with her triumphantly exerting your powers, charming the world, carrying everything before you" (VIII, 338–
39). Verena saw hitherto unsuspected truths in such a response; Miriam is not as easily persuaded. She turns Peter's
proposal back on him: he has always been interested in the
theater, he has encouraged and helped her, why doesn't he
give up his career for her? Miriam's request makes so little
sense—there is nothing Peter could do for art or for her any
more if he did give up his career—that I think we must
understand it as her attempt to put Peter in her position
and so make him understand why she cannot give up her
work.[13] But he cannot understand. His joking suggestion
that marriage is impossible because "Our ambitions are in-
ferior and odious, but we're tied fast to them" (VIII, 256) is
truer than he knows. The lovers are brought to an impasse.

As James develops this final conflict between Miriam and
Peter, he follows his study of the *"nature d'actrice"* to its inevitable conclusion. Miriam makes a calculated marriage of
convenience and then goes on to triumph on stage, ironically as Juliet, a woman who dies for love. And Peter, who
returns to London in time to witness this performance, finally accepts the rightness of Miriam's decision: "Miriam
Rooth was sublime.... Peter Sherringham, though he saw
but a fragment of the performance, read clear, at the last, in
the intense light of genius with which this fragment was
charged, that even so after all he had been rewarded for his
formidable journey. The great trouble of his infatuation
subsided, leaving behind it something appreciably deep
and pure" (VIII, 437–38). He is at last free to make a
proper marriage for a diplomat, and he turns to Biddy
Dormer.

We have no way of knowing at what point James hit upon
his parallel plot, the Nick Dormer–Julia Dallow story.
Given the title of the book and James's long-standing interest in the character of the actress, we are probably correct in

assuming that the Miriam-Peter story came first.[14] This story, as we have seen, poses the conflicts of art and "the world" and of men and women in irreconcilable terms—and interestingly, finds a satisfying resolution to such conflicts. Yet it is a rather thin story: the conflicts are lesser than those raised in *The Bostonians*; the theatrical concerns relatively unimportant as compared with the political vision at the heart of *The Princess Casamassima*. It is hard not to feel that the opposition of art and "the world" and the "latent antagonism of the sexes" should have led to more; perhaps James's extreme indebtedness to the work of Black and Mrs. Ward hampered him. The parallel plot that he added to what they had suggested somewhat deepens the resonance of that story by retelling it in slightly different terms so that compromise is tested as a possible solution to the issues in conflict. But something still is missing.

One difficulty is that the claims of art in the parallel plot are not adequately realized. To some extent, this is the result of a problem that does not arise in the case of the actress whose work is largely visible. In one part of the preface to *The Tragic Muse* that we can trust, James remarks on the difficulty encountered in depicting the artist: "My presentation of the artist *in triumph* must be flat in proportion as it really sticks to its subject—it can only smuggle in relief and variety. For, to put the matter in an image, all we then—in his triumph—see of the charm-compeller is the back he turns to us as he bends over his work. 'His' triumph, decently, is but the triumph of what he produces, and that is another affair" (VII, xxi). The introduction of the aesthete, Gabriel Nash, as Nick Dormer's companion and guiding spirit—as the spokesman for art and, implicitly, celibacy—is one way in which James added "relief and variety" to his depiction of the artist, though he did so at the cost of trivializing the claims of art. He was willing to do this, I would guess, not only because Nash helped him to dramatize the

undramatic but also because the inclusion of Nash constituted yet another claim for popular attention, since aestheticism was another major artistic preoccupation of the
eighties and the aesthete frequently appeared as a character
in the work of popular writers as well as in the work of
minority writers.

Critics have made much of possible life models for Nash
but generally failed to recognize that he, like many of
James's characters, is based on familiar literary types.[15] We
can distinguish two versions of the aesthete in the fiction of
the eighties; Nash combines elements of both. One type of
aesthete approaches life as a field for the artist to work in
and does not hesitate to manipulate others in order to grat-
ify his senses. This figure was of special interest to the minority artist who understood the attractions and dangers of
the aesthetic movement and marshaled his forces to resist.
Robert Buchanan, remembered now for applying the
phrase "the Fleshly School of Poetry" to the Pre-Raphaelites
in the seventies, concluded in the eighties that the English
poets were not so immoral as he had thought and that the
real enemy was the soulless French aesthete. The villain in
his novel *The Martyrdom of Madeline* (1882) is consequently a
Frenchman, a poet, self-described as "an artiste—in affairs
of gallantry as in all others,"[16] which is to say that his sexual
immorality is a function of an artistic taste developed at the
expense of his conscience. Vernon Lee (Violet Paget) dedicated her novel on the subject, *Miss Brown* (1884), to Henry
James, much to his embarrassment. This is the story of a
selfish, shallow, amoral painter-poet who "enjoyed playing
upon a living soul" and so educates a young woman with
the intention of creating an ideal wife for himself.[17] John
Davidson's amusing book *The North Wall* (1885) raises a serious issue through a fictional artist who, unable to sell his
written work, creates a novel in life by impersonating another man and wreaking near havoc in his family. The artist

"justifies" himself: "we [artists in life] shall be granted, I doubt not, the most cordial permission to execute atrocities which, committed selfishly, would brand the criminal as an unnatural monster, but which, performed for art's sake, will redound everlastingly to the credit of the artist."[18]

The philosophic and moral questions raised by the aesthete who is an artist in life could not have been of much interest to the general public. But the extravagant personal poses which the aesthete sometimes adopted in an effort to make his own life into a work of art did amuse and interest many people, and the second type of aesthete, the poseur, strangely garbed and given to paradoxes and oracular utterances, entered the popular domain in a variety of forms in the eighties.[19] Gilbert and Sullivan's *Patience* (1881) good-humoredly mocked aesthetic taste through its songs and dialogue, satirized Wilde and Swinburne in the characters of the rival aesthetes, and cleverly adapted the work of Burne-Jones and Whistler in the costumes of the lovesick maidens. George Du Maurier created Messrs. Maudle and Postlethwaite, a painter and poet respectively, and Mrs. Cimabue Brown, "the priestess of the aesthetic cult," in the early eighties— "the most brilliant episode of his long connection with 'Punch,'" a delighted James wrote.[20] Even the most conventional of novelists with no serious interest in the aesthetic movement included such poseurs in their works in deference to popular taste. Rhoda Broughton's *Second Thoughts* (1880), for example, is a sentimental love story about a young woman who comes to love a man whom she at first disliked intensely. One of her suitors is a morbid poet who, by contrast to the healthy-minded heroine, provides moments of comedy but serves no real function in the book. David Christie Murray's *The Weaker Vessel* (1888) is a similar example. This too is a sentimental romance in which a young man makes an unfortunate marriage and then falls in love with the girl he should have married. The two aesthetes in the novel (who are largely irrelevant to the plot) moralize continually about redeeming mankind through beauty but prove themselves incapable of simple human sympathy.[21]

James, as I have indicated, knew both the aesthete as manipulator and as poseur. In "The Author of Beltraffio" (1884), he played them off against each other—"He was the original and she the inevitable imitation" (XVI, 25), James's narrator informs us describing Mark Ambient, the writer, and his affected sister—and then added an ironic twist by exposing the puritanical Mrs. Ambient as the real manipulator, while Ambient proves to be quite innocuous. In Gabriel Nash, James again revealed his sympathy for the aesthete. Here he combined the two roles: it is as the poseur that Nash shocks Nick's straitlaced family by responding to Biddy's question, "Are you then an aesthete?" with, "Merely to be is such a *metier*; to live such an art; to feel such a career!" (VII, 33); as the manipulator, he responds to Julia's question, "Are you an artist?" with, "I try to be…but I work in such difficult material…. I work in life!" (VII, 152–53). In this double role he exemplifies and promotes a principle of self-realization that Nick must accept if he is to become an artist. Unfortunately, Nash's comic manner, while successfully mitigating the sinister implications of his approach to life, also robs him of the weight such a serious principle should carry in the book.

Because of her singlemindedness, "the world" is neither stumbling block nor temptation to Miriam; for Nick, who is deeply ambivalent about himself, it is both. He is one of James's many weak males; unlike Peter, conciliation always comes more easily to him than confrontation. He finds "the world" arrayed against him in the persons of his mother and sisters, who look to him to succeed in politics where his father failed and thereby save them from obscurity and poverty; of Mr. Carteret, his father's childless friend, approaching death and eager to name Nick his heir if only Nick will pursue a political career; and of his cousin Julia Dallow, whose wealth, passion, and political ambition (necessarily vicarious) are formidable weapons. Her hopes for Nick are at once selfish and generous: "the cause of her interest in him was partly the vision of his helping her to the particular extensions she did desire—the taste and thrill of great affairs and of public action. To have such ambitions for him appeared to her the greatest honour she could do him..." (VII, 148–49). Nor is Nick an entirely unwilling victim. Though he dreams of becoming a portrait painter (portraiture, it should be noted, was the kind of painting James valued most), cowardice alone does not prevent him from urging the claims of art. He is moved enough by the "sense of England" (VII, 291), his familial obligations, and his passion for Julia to stand for election— with her financial backing, in her home county. He wins the election; he proposes to Julia; he calls on Mr. Carteret—and the inevitable reaction sets in: "It was plain that he was not fated to go in for independence; the most that he could treat himself to would be dependence that was duly grateful" (VII, 304).

Nash is hardly an adequate counterbalance to the forces arrayed against Nick. In the beginning of the book, when Nick's family meets Nash in Paris, Nick tells Nash what he means to him: "At Oxford you were very bad company for me—my evil genius: you opened my eyes, you communicated the poison. Since then, little by little, it has been working within me; vaguely, covertly, insensibly at first, but during the last year or two with violence, pertinacity, cruelty. I've resorted to every antidote in life; but it's no use— I'm stricken" (VII, 182). Yet we are aware of the subversive power of art only through the discomfort Nash's manner arouses in Nick's family, and since we do not feel the power of art Nick claims to feel, we are not surprised that he goes on to stand for Parliament in spite of his brave declaration.

Nash intervenes more energetically in Nick's life after the election, when Nick has taken some time off to paint. He enthusiastically praises Nick's work and speaks eloquently of the need to realize one's deepest inclinations, "To be what one *may* be" (VIII, 26). It is talk, James observes, that "marked really—if the question be of noting the exact point—a turn in the tide of Nick Dormer's personal situation" (VIII, 23). But we do not really feel it as such. Instead, the moment that seems to signal a change in Nick's life is the moment Julia enters his studio and finds him painting Miriam Rooth. While the sitting was arranged by Nash, who believes that the example of the actress pursuing her career and the opportunity afforded by her sitting will inspire his friend, the impact of the scene does not derive from his agency in it but from Nick's forced confrontation with the women who vividly represent the two sides of his conflict. As Nick tries to conciliate Julia, he is aware of Miriam: "She seemed somehow in easy possession of the place, and even at that instant Nick noted how handsome she looked; so that he said to himself inaudibly, in some deeper depth of consciousness, 'How I should like to paint her *that* way!'" (VIII, 56). The intimacy of the artists— because they are artists together—demonstrates, in a way that all of Nash's talk cannot, the spell art holds for the artist. It also scares Julia and leads to her breaking off her engagement with Nick and so to his resigning his seat in Parliament. While the incorporation of Miriam in the story at this point helps us unify the novel by suggesting an affinity of spirit between the two artists, it also testifies to James's recognition that Nash, acting and speaking alone, is inadequate as an embodiment of art.

Though dramatically occasioned, the breach between Nick and Julia is not permanent. The values of "the world," Nick's hesitant nature, and the demands of a contrasting plot prohibit a permanent separation. So James hints at a final compromise. Nash returns one last time after Nick has undertaken work as an artist in earnest. The aesthete is nervous and ill at ease: in his role as manipulator, he has moved Nick as much as he can hope to; in his role as poseur, he is disturbed by Nick's unembarrassed willingness to confront the practical difficulties entailed by the pursuit of his vocation. Before he disappears completely from Nick's life, Nash predicts that Nick and Julia will be reunited. However, a new union must be different from the old: because Nick has asserted his independence, a more equal relationship must result from reunion. Nick can never go back to being Julia's "member" (VII, 243), a word his mother supplies, to his embarrassment, in conscious reference to his political victory. Nash, who is always an astute judge of people, recognizes how deeply Nick is drawn to Julia and her values in spite of his break with her, and he tells Nick that Julia will ask him to paint her picture and then, "Your differences with the beautiful lady will be patched up, and you'll each come round a little and meet the other halfway. The beautiful lady will swallow your profession if you'll swallow hers. She'll put up with the palette if you put up with the country-house" (VIII, 406). Although the novel does not end with Nick's marriage to Julia, it does end with most of Nash's prophecy having come true: Nick paints Julia's picture and entertains her country house guests by doing pictures of them. And a rival suitor to Julia, a man with a promising political future, is rumored to have "ceased...to believe in her" (VIII, 411). In this resolution, we see an alternative solution to "The essential, latent antagonism of the sexes...founded on irreconcilable interests." While Peter and Miriam each pursue their own careers and accept the fact that they must give each other up, Nick and Julia both will compromise theirs in order to retain their personal relationship.

I am aware that by discussing *The Tragic Muse* in terms of

its relationship to the theatrical novels of Mrs. Ward and William Black and the aesthetic novel of the eighties, I have emphasized the extent to which the book divides into two distinct stories. But a discussion that focused on James's other important concern in this book, the difficulties between the sexes, would falsely suggest a more unified novel.[22] James seems to have conceived his book first in terms of the two separate subjects, and most readers are troubled by the extent to which his two plots function independently of one another. Perhaps James's sense that this book would be another popular failure made it impossible for him to commit himself fully to it. The unsatisfying treatment of his subject as well as his difficulties with the two plots suggest a failure of energy or enthusiasm more than anything else. Still, *The Tragic Muse* is a richer and more suggestive novel than the other books I have named here. Apart from simply encompassing more by virtue of telling two stories, James's novel sensitively judges the differing ways in which the claims of passion and talent might be settled. Miriam and Nash, the actress and the aesthete, both speak eloquently of the necessity of realizing one's potential and so being true to one's self. Their voices are so strong, in fact, that we must distrust Nick's and Julia's willingness to compromise. In spite of immediate pain, Miriam and Peter, in pursuing their own ways, seem to be happier at the end of the book than Nick and Julia will ever be. That James does not describe the terms these two finally settle on is suggestive of the continuing tensions which will characterize their relationship. It is no wonder that James's contemporaries found this unsentimental book unappealing; nor is it any wonder that in spite of its being so much part of the eighties, the book speaks cogently enough to us now to make us wish James had been able to do more with his subject.

FIVE

Responses to Failure

True to what he had written Stevenson, *The Tragic Muse* was James's last long novel for a number of years. Though he had not yet given up hope of making himself felt in the marketplace, he was ready for a change, and he turned to the drama and the short story. Leon Edel has told and retold the story of James's interest in the theater from his childhood on. His venture into playwriting, accompanied by dreams of commanding a large audience, was in part a means of compensating for feelings of impotence first after his mother's death and then in a much greater degree after the popular failures of his next three novels, and in part it was an attempt to make money.[1] After his mother's death, James recast "Daisy Miller" as a play and began a dramatization of *The American*. This was abandoned until Edward Compton offered to back the play. James resumed work on it and now further goaded by the dwindling interest in his novels decided to try his hand at about half a dozen plays (in an exuberant mood it was "half a dozen—a dozen, five dozen" [*N*, p. 99]) in order to provide himself with a fair test of his skill as a dramatist. He gave five years, an unrecorded number of scenarios, and six plays (only two of which were produced: *The American* in 1891 and *Guy Domville* in 1895) to the theater; that was enough for him to fail the test. It was also enough to dispel his naiveté about his popular appeal.

Abstractly considered, a decision to write for the stage was not a bad one. The well-made play with its complicated stage business and fixed characters dominated the English stage well into the nineties.[2] The form was old, but if a playwright had the sense of the ridiculous that Brandon Thomas brought to *Charley's Aunt* (1892) or the genius for witticism that Oscar Wilde brought to *The Importance of Being Earnest* (1895), he could turn it into an attractive, salable article. At the same time, a real change was coming. In his articles on the London stage from the late seventies through the eighties as well as in *The Tragic Muse*, James had remarked on the poverty of contemporary English drama. In "After the Play" (1889), a dialogue on the contemporary English theater, he observed that London life in particular offered a rich field for the dramatist: "If the occasion always produced the man London would have produced an Aristophanes."[3] Shortly after James wrote this, the occasion did produce the man—or men. Henry Arthur Jones and Arthur Wing Pinero, responding to the example of Ibsen, brought serious social issues to the stage in the mid-nineties. Their plays look timid to us today, and it is easy to be scornful of them. Holbrook Jackson, for example, comments on how cautiously Jones and Pinero followed Ibsen's lead: "Obviously, the game would be to hearten realism with a dash of sentimentalism; in short, to water down Ibsen; not to declare that 'it is right to do something hitherto regarded as infamous' (*vide* G. B. S.), but to treat seriously, in a play with no specific purpose, something hitherto considered as naughty and therefore only deserving of facetious comment, and to call it a 'problem play.'"[4] Still, the "problem play" aroused a new popular interest in the theater and became a kind of equivalent of the best seller. Without it, George Bernard Shaw's work in the second half of the nineties probably would have been impossible.

The author who could revitalize the well-made play or tap the new interest in the "problem play" could make a great deal of money. Even novelists like F. Marion Crawford and Walter Besant who were making money with their books spoke wistfully of the financial attractions of the theater. Crawford, after finding parallels between the novel and the play in *The Novel: What It Is,* observed, "We [novelists] are not genuine playwriters for many reasons; chiefly, perhaps, because we are not clever enough, since a successful play is incomparably more lucrative than a successful novel."[5] Besant, in *The Pen and the Book* (1899), a book of advice for the aspiring writer, spoke of the drama as a promising field because of growing contemporary interest in the theater and the consequently improved "pecuniary position" of the dramatist: "His income may thus already surpass, and will, very soon, most certainly surpass, that possible in any of the 'learned' professions. The successful dramatist of the future will be far more successful, if we think of income, than will be possible for the physician or lawyer."[6] Crawford's and Besant's concern with income follows logically from their shared conviction that writing is a trade and that the writer's responsibility is to satisfy his customers. That James spoke so frequently and so longingly of making money as a playwright is an indication of a frustration deep-seated enough to make him forget for a time his conviction that the artist must serve himself first.

Certainly James's eagerness to comply with what he believed to be the expectations of theater managers accounts in good part for his failure as a playwright. He did learn to appreciate Ibsen and particularly to value the very quality which separated Ibsen's work from the well-made play—as he observed in his essay on *Hedda Gabler* (1891), Ibsen's drama is "essentially that supposedly undramatic thing, the picture not of an action but of a condition. It is the portrait of a nature, the story of what Paul Bourget would call an *état d'âme,* and of a state of nerves as well as of soul, a state of temper, of disappointment, of desperation."[7] But he was unable to follow Ibsen's lead. Instead, he remained bound to the form he had learned from the French theater. Most of his plays, including the adaptations of his fiction, are distressingly lifeless well-made plays. Only in *The Reprobate* (1891) and *Guy Domville* (written 1893) did he attempt "the portrait of a nature," but in neither play was he able to free himself sufficiently from the constricting stage business of the well-made play for a new intention to stand forth convincingly. In the preface to his second collection of *Theatricals* (1895), a volume containing *The Album* (1891) and *The Reprobate,* published after he recognized that these plays would never see production and after he had given up trying to write for the stage, James spoke of his attempts to meet the demands of the theater. He said he had believed the trick was to produce something short and simple, something possessing "the bland air of the little domestic fairy-tale": "The different fairies had to be summoned to the cradle, from the fairy Genial to the fairy Coincidence, and one was not to feel the omens propitious till the scheme bristled with as many of these old friends as a nursery-tale.... Then the mixture was to be stirred to the tune of perpetual motion and served, under pain of being rejected with disgust, with the time honored bread-sauce of the happy ending." In retrospect, he believed that he had probably been too timid—"the question, in the face of overestimated chances, ultimately came up [in reconsidering the plays for publication] of whether the dread of supersubtlety had not weighed too much."[8]

James's professed fear of rejection is so excessive here that it is hard not to believe that he was also trying to cover a second difficulty. The reticence that prevailed in his fiction operated with equal force when he turned to the drama. This was particularly unfortunate, for the theater did not allow the subterfuges the novel did, and James could not deal as delicately and indirectly with sex as he was used to doing—and he avoided the subject. Next to the popular "problem play," James's plays appear old-fashioned. *The Other House* (1896) underlines this difficulty. The work was intended originally as a play; a scenario was put together early in 1894 but was rejected by Compton and set aside. When Clement Shorter offered James space in the *Illustrated London News*, James eagerly accepted. Always in search of new readers, he wrote Shorter, "I should...like to capture the public of the *Illustrated News*," and he anticipated that *The Other House* would serve well: "I shall endeavour to be thrilling, and my material is such that I think I shall succeed."[9] The book was thrilling, involving the rivalry between two women for the love of a widower and the murder of his child by one of the women, but it was not popular. Contemporary reviewers praised the unaccustomed directness with which James had approached his subject and the amount of action he had infused in it. But, as one noted, while the book represented a changed manner for its author, "The change has no reference...to what are imagined to be the tastes of the circulating libraries."[10] As with his plays, in this novel based on a play, James had eschewed the new. *The Other House* is old-fashioned melodrama. Lacking the topicality of the "problem play" and not dealing with any other topical issue, it could not appeal to the mass market as James had hoped.

While James struggled with stage managers and scenarios, he continued to write short stories as he had from the beginning of his career. Like the drama, the short story was approaching a period of revitalization. The increasing fragmentation of the reading public had led to a proliferation of new magazines ranging from popular weeklies, supported heavily by advertising and sold at newsstands, to avant-garde little magazines. The short story flourished in the new magazines—a reflection, no doubt, of the newsstand magazine publisher's awareness that his readership might vary from week to week and the little magazine publisher's fear that the next issue might be a long time coming. H. G. Wells, whose own career as a fiction writer began in the nineties with the short story, recalled the period as an exuberant one for both authors and critics: "The 'nineties was a good and stimulating period for a short story writer.... No short story of the slightest distinction went for long unrecognized. The sixpenny popular magazines had still to deaden down the conception of what a short story might be to the imaginative limitation of the common reader—and a maximum length of six thousand words. Short stories broke out everywhere.... People talked about them tremendously, compared them, and ranked them. That was the thing that mattered."[11]

Yet James apparently felt no such enthusiasm for the possibilities open to him. He carefully sought out new markets but noted a loss of the old. When he wrote to Howells after the opening of *Guy Domville* bemoaning his "evil days" and looking to the resumption of his literary career, he tried to reconcile himself to forgoing magazine serialization in the future. He complained (with some exaggeration as it turned out), "what is clear is that periodical publication is practically closed to me—I'm the last hand that the magazines, in this country or in the U.S., seem to want." He cited his experience of the past several years as proof of his assertion and listed the magazines and publishers that had ignored him: *Scribner's*, the *Century, Cosmopolitan,* the *Atlantic,* Houghton Mifflin, and Macmillan.[12] In lamenting the disappearance of his old markets, James was mourning his exclusion from the magazines that he regarded as the arbiters of culture,[13] sensing the end of his dream of being an accepted spokesman for a wide popular audience. He erred, as we can recognize, in overestimating the influence of the monthly magazines and in blaming himself alone for the exclusion from their pages. With the changes in the reading public as the century progressed, the magazines that James listed had become increasingly timid publishers of fiction. Dependent on subscriptions and aware of their diminished influence in a diverse market, they were unwilling to risk offending potential readers. A writer who failed to observe genteel standards or who made too many intellectual demands on his readers might well find traditional markets closed to him.[14] But James in 1895 had just begun to recognize the diversity of the reading public—the letter to Howells that I quote here is the one in which he observes that "A new generation...has taken universal possession"—and he was not yet ready to trace out the implications of that recognition.

Given James's absorption in the theater and his unhappiness about the literary marketplace in the early nineties, it is not surprising that most of the stories he wrote in this period are not particularly successful. Many of these were tales of the supernatural, a cliché-ridden genre that had been given a new vogue by the study of folklore, the work of the Society for Psychical Research (SPR, founded in 1882), and the revival of spiritualism,[15] and a new vehicle of dissemination in the currently popular short story.[16] For the most part, James's supernatural stories were potboilers, often carelessly written but shrewdly enough timed and placed to attract popular attention. With the exception of "The Friends of the Friends," a slightly later story (1896, published as "The Way It Came" in the *Chap-book* and *Chapman's Magazine of Fiction*), these stories were published in the old monthlies or in the new weeklies, magazines of fairly wide circulation. Two of them, "Sir Edmund Orme" (1891, in *Black and White*) and "Owen Wingrave" (1892, in the *Graphic*) were placed in Christmas issues to take advantage of both the general interest in the genre and the English tradition of ghost stories at Christmastime. They differ markedly from the Hawthornian ghost stories of James's early career—"The Romance of Certain Old Clothes" (1868), "The Ghostly Rental" (1876). Their tone is less brooding, their interest less moral. Instead, they are built on contemporary notions of psychic phenomena. "Sir Dominick Ferrand" (1892, published in *Cosmopolitan* as "Jersey Villas") deals with a case of mental telepathy; "The Private Life" (1892, in the *Atlantic*), with the phenomenon of split personality; while the ghost stories proper show James's knowledge of what the Society for Psychical Research called "veridical apparitions" or "attested phantasms."[17]

James's later comments on ghost stories afford a useful perspective from which to judge these stories. In the New York Edition preface to "The Turn of the Screw," he commented on the literary implications of the work of the SPR in demystifying the supernatural by describing ghostly deportment and dress in detail: "The new type [of ghost story] indeed, the mere modern 'psychical' case, washed clean of all queerness as by exposure to a flowing laboratory tap, and equipped with credentials vouching for this—the new type clearly promised little, for the more it was respectably certified the less it seemed of a nature to rouse the dear old sacred terror" (XII, xv). Perhaps James was recalling John Kendrick Bangs's numerous ghost stories which had appeared in *Harper's Weekly* in the nineties along with his own "London" letters and *The Awkward Age*.[18] Bangs's stories generally deal with a narrator-percipient eager to add his experience to the growing body of ghostly encounters. The ghosts in the stories possess the human characteristics of SPR ghosts (in addition to which, they talk) and as a result cannot evoke the terror or wonder associated with the traditional ghost story. Indeed, they tend to be comic or charming more often than not.

But if an author could forgo the impulse to documentation and concentrate on the percipient rather than the apparition, he could create effective ghost stories that still satisfied modern tastes. We see successful instances in the work of some of James's friends. Stevenson, who wrote a number of stories of the supernatural, wrote one that is truly a ghost story, "Markheim" (1885). The ghost in this story never assumes a definitive shape or identity, but he moves the murderer Markheim to turn himself in, and we can interpret him as conscience personified or an agent of God. Kipling's ghosts are psychological rather than spiritual. His most popular ghost story, "The Phantom 'Rickshaw" (1888), traces a man's mental and physical decline as he repeatedly encounters a phantom rickshaw carrying a woman whom he had treated badly. The absence of moralistic language makes the story a study of an obsession rather than a case of conscience. "At the End of the Passage" (1890), praised by James as "a perfect little piece of hard representation" and as a story type for which he felt "a latent relish," details the mental collapse—signaled by visions of his own ghostly double—and death of an army officer in India.[19] H. G. Wells, in "The Red Room" (1896), depicts an initially skeptical narrator-protagonist who spends a night in a "haunted" room, only to discover that it is himself and not a ghost that is to be feared: "The worst of all things that haunt poor mortal man" is "Fear...that deafens and darkens and overwhelms."[20] In the New York Edition preface to the volume containing most of the ghost stories, James spoke of the advantage gained by a focus on the percipient: "the safest arena for the play of moving accidents and mighty mutations and strange encounters, or whatever odd matters, is the field, as I may call it, rather of their second than of their first exhibition. By which...I mean nothing more cryptic than I feel myself show them best by showing almost exclusively the way they are felt, by recognising as their main interest some impression strongly made by them and intensely received" (XVII, xix). But it was not until "The Turn of the Screw" (1898), written after James had reestablished himself as a novelist, that is, at a time of reduced professional anxiety, that he was able to write a story in which he really did justice to the idea he expresses here.

In the earlier ghost stories of the nineties, the ghostly encounter is typically a gratuitous acknowledgment of popular taste rather than the center of the story. In "Sir Edmund Orme," James creates a provocative situation with a narrator more interested in the mother of the girl he is courting than in the girl herself and a mother too eager to marry off her daughter. But he deflects our attention from this serious issue by introducing the ghost of Sir Edmund Orme to precipitate the narrator's engagement. Like Bangs's ghosts, Orme is a charming figure pictured in his "first exhibition," fully justifying the narrator's observation that "ghosts were much less alarming and much more amusing than was commonly supposed" (XVII, 390). In "Owen Wingrave" so much space is devoted to the delineation of the clash between Owen with his pacifist inclinations and his family and friends with their militaristic values that the encounter with the ghost seems merely a perfunctory end to the story rather than its climax. The story is further weakened by James's careless handling of the supernatural: it is not clear who or what kills Owen. His murderous ancestor, "sometimes seen" (XVII, 300) as a ghost, should be a chastened spirit now and therefore not the cause of Owen's death—yet the force that killed the wicked ancestor cannot logically be blamed for the death of the pacifist Owen either. And even in the more carefully written story, "The Friends of the Friends," the jealousy with which the narrator regards her fiancé's relationship with her friend is of central importance, while the ghostly encounter—in which she does not share—is again secondary. In this story, too, there is the gratuitous gesture: the narrator insists that her fiancé never really met her friend but saw a wraith instead, an explanation soothing to her jealousy and dignified by her modern notion that it would be "gratifying to be the subject of one of those inexplicable occurrences that are chronicled in thrilling books and disputed about at learned meetings" (XVII, 358).

The distress indicated by the indifferent writing in the ghost stories finally came to an end with the greater distress of the opening night of *Guy Domville* and the subsequent release from pressure that enabled James to devote his full attention to fiction once more. I do not want to minimize the frustration, the unhappiness, and the final personal humiliation that James's pursuit of fame in the theater cost him. But James had the gifts of resiliency and self-confidence; when he tended to bravado in the face of pain and failure, as he often did, it was because he was a survivor. When he wrote to Howells complaining of falling on "evil days," he also insisted, "I mean to do far better work than ever I have done before. I have, potentially, improved immensely and am bursting with ideas and subjects...." A day later, he recorded a promise to himself in his notebook: "I take up my *own* old pen again—the pen of all my old unforgettable efforts and sacred struggles. To myself—today—I need say no more. Large and full and high the future still opens. It is now indeed that I may do the work of my life. And I will" (*N*, p. 179). When he wrote to William describing the "cruel ordeal" of the opening night of *Guy Domville*, he asserted that he was "rapidly and resolutely" recovering from his disappointment and consequent depression, and he concluded his letter defiantly: "I am not plangent—one must take the thick with the thin—and I have such possibilities of another and better sort before me."[21] And James's friend Edmund Gosse suggests that James's buoyancy was more than an empty pose. He recalls James's wildly fluctuating moods as he courted theater managers, his extreme tension as the opening of *Guy Domville* approached, and his great change the next morning: "The discipline of toiling for the caprices of the theatre had amounted, for so redundant an imaginative writer, to the putting on of a mental strait-jacket.... He vibrated [now] with the sense of release, and he began to enjoy, physically and intellectually, a freedom which had hitherto been foreign to his nature."[22] Edel disputes Gosse's recollection, citing evidence to suggest that James was more upset and exhausted than Gosse claims.[23] But if Gosse misremembered the morning after the play, it does not follow that he misremembered James's general reaction to failure.

In evaluating James's response to failure, psychological critics have been particularly unwilling to take James at his word. Edmund Wilson, looking at James's work in the late nineties (including *What Maisie Knew* and *The Awkward Age*), argued long ago that this fiction was marked by the author's "subsidence back into himself." At this point in his career, Wilson claimed, "It has...become difficult for James to sustain his old objectivity: he has relapsed into a dreamy interior world, where values are often uncertain and where it is not even possible any longer for him to judge his effect on his audience...."[24] Maxwell Geismar has maliciously enlarged Wilson's point, deriding James's technical achievements in the nineties as a neurotic form of compensation and dwelling on his "infantile" identification with the numerous young protagonists who now appear in his fiction and who are viewed as isolated from and morally superior to the corrupt society that had rejected their creator.[25] Leon Edel has provided us with a more sympathetic psychological interpretation of James's work in the late nineties. Observing the preoccupations with unrealized expectations and betrayed innocence that seem to characterize James's work in this period even more than they had earlier, he theorizes: "At this moment of defeat [after *Guy Domville*] Henry James seized the skills of his 'technique' as if they were a lifebelt, and indulged in a vigorous and mature inquiry into forms he had not hitherto questioned. Simultaneously we have an emotional retreat [signaled by his subject matter]—that retreat of which man is capable in order to nurse and heal his spiritual as well as physical wounds."[26] With this premise, Edel interprets the work of the nineties as an intuitive form of self-therapy, arguing that as James's child protagonists grow successively older with each novel, James is in effect growing up again and thereby healing himself.[27] None of these critics considers James's post-theater work in the same context that I have here. To do so, as we will see, is to recognize that James's work in the later nineties is not as idiosyncratic as these critics imply. If we are to apply the term "regressive" to these works, we must do so cautiously, with an awareness of the literary context they come from.

Critics whose central concern is James's formal achievements begin with James's attempt to find something in his experience in the theater that would justify the brave claims he made for the future in his letters after the opening of *Guy Domville*. A few weeks after the letters, James devoted a long notebook entry to what he could take from his experience:

Compensations and solutions seem to stand there with open arms for me—and something of the "meaning" to come to me of past bitterness, of recent bitterness that otherwise has seemed a mere sickening, unflavoured draught. Has a *part* of all this wasted passion and squandered time (of the last 5 years) been simply the precious lesson, taught me in that roundabout and devious, that cruelly expensive, way, *of the singular value for a narrative plan too* of the...divine principle of the Scenario? If that *has* been one side of the moral of the whole unspeakable, the whole tragic experience, I almost bless the pangs and the pains and the miseries of it.... IF, I say, I have crept round through long apparent barrenness, through suffering and sadness intolerable, to that rare perception—why my infinite little loss is converted to an almost infinite little gain. [*N*, p. 188]

Although James speaks tentatively, almost wistfully, here, he is enunciating a principle that was to have great consequences for his fiction in the future. F. O. Matthiessen and Kenneth Murdock, the editors of the notebooks, cite the passage I have just quoted in their introduction and then go on to observe that the works that followed immediately upon this recognition, *The Spoils of Poynton* (1897) and *What Maisie Knew*, "form the pivotal point between his [James's] earlier and later methods" (*N*, p. xviii) because of their dependence on a dramatic or scenic method of presentation. Leo Levy, in *Versions of Melodrama*, after discussing James's persistent concern with irreconcilable moral states and his difficulties in finding an adequate form for his concerns, suggests that in the fiction following the drama, "The final integration of vision with the limiting formal principle of drama makes possible James's emergence as a truly effective melodramatist."[28] The two books devoted exclusively to James's work in the nineties, Walter Isle's *Experiments in Form* and Joseph Wiesenfarth's *Henry James and the Dramatic Analogy*, at the risk of making substance secondary to form, explore James's use of specific dramatic techniques in his novels as do numerous articles on the individual works in the period. It is true, as all these critics make us aware, that the fiction following the plays is characterized by a concision and balance lacking in James's earlier work and that we frequently have the sense of witnessing the story unfold as we read, for we see events through a carefully controlled, limited perspective and we hear dialogue in which every word advances action or reveals character. But here again consideration of the popular context of James's work is missing. That consideration will temper the claims of these critics too: James's work in the late nineties is as profoundly influenced by the fiction of his contemporaries as by the drama and, as my discussion of *The Awkward Age* will show, some of what seems to be derived from the drama appears in the work of those literary contemporaries as well.

Critical failure to think of James in terms of his long engagement with the marketplace has also obscured another lesson made emphatically clear by his experience in the theater. James was finally forced to recognize his place as a minority writer. We have seen that he observed to Howells that "a new generation" had "taken universal possession" and so acknowledged the mass market. In a second letter to William after the opening of *Guy Domville*, he discussed the public response to his play in a way that further revealed a changed perception: "As for the play, in three words, it has been, I think I may say, a rare and distinguished private success and scarcely anything at all of a public one. By a private success, I mean with the even moderately cultivated, civilised and intelligent *individual*, with 'people of taste' in short, of almost any kind, as distinguished from the vast English Philistine mob—the regular 'theatrical public' of London, which, of all the vulgar publics London contains, is the most brutishly and densely vulgar."[29] Of course this is excessive and defensive, but the distinctions—really those of highbrow and lowbrow—are valid. James's further conclusion, that only a narrow segment of the heterogeneous audience was his, marks the end of his expectations of popular success.

This discovery of his role and the necessary change in expectations was further explored in the cluster of short stories that James wrote in the mid-nineties, the tales of literary life. The outburst in the letter to William angrily affirms or crystallizes an understanding more temperately expressed in the fiction. James made a point of the personal element in this work. Most of the tales of literary life were collected in two volumes—*Terminations* (1895; including "The Death of the Lion," "The Coxon Fund," and "The Middle Years") and *Embarrassments* (1896; including "The Figure in the Carpet" and "The Next Time")—volumes whose titles point to the feelings of failure and shame that are examined in these stories of unappreciated authors. Later James filled one and one-half volumes of the New York Edition with tales of literary life and noted in one of the prefaces, "the material for any picture of personal states so specifically complicated as those of my hapless friends in the present volume will have been drawn preponderantly from the depths of the designer's own mind.... the states represented, the embarrassments and predicaments studied, the tragedies and comedies recorded, can be intelligently fathered but on his own intimate experience" (XV, ix). Still later, James gave the name of one of these stories to a volume of his autobiography—*The Middle Years*.

It is not surprising that this title should have had a special meaning for James. The story titled "The Middle Years" (1893, in *Scribner's*) is a self-indulgent piece about a neglected writer who longs for a second chance in life to make good his expectations of himself. He is befriended by a young man whose love enables him to see that "The thing is to have made somebody care" (XVI, 105). This leads to an acceptance of what his life has been: "We work in the dark— we do what we can—we give what we have. Our doubt is our passion and our passion is our task. The rest is the madness of art" (XVI, 105). While the defense of the artist's life with its risks and uncertainties is important to James, the assurance that a small audience is enough if it is truly receptive is particularly important now. The impassioned eloquence of the artist's remarks also suggests something more: a permissible transference seems to be at work, for the artist's language is the language of love inspired by another man, apparently a confession of personal need surfacing at a difficult time in James's life.[30]

Less than a year after writing "The Middle Years," James planned another story about an artist who feels himself a failure, this time casting it in heterosexual terms, a change that suggests an increased command over his feelings. His notebook outline is more complete than is usual with the tales of literary life, but he never wrote the story. It is a fable of artistic death and rebirth in which popular success is damned as prostitution of one's talent, or more precisely, as a kind of emasculation. The small but receptive audience appears again as a regenerative force:

> A young man who has dreamed that he has the genius of a poet...makes, in the political milieu, a worldly, showy, advantageous marriage, a marriage that pushes him, commits him, vulgarizes him, destroys his faith in his faculty. He forsakes, for this end, a girl whom he has originally loved and who is poor and intelligent. She has been the confidante of his literary, his poetic dreams; she has listened to his verses, believed in his genius and his future. He breaks with her, in an hour of temptation, and casts his lot the other way.... The woman he marries has taken him away; but he has died, as it were, in her hands. His corpse is politically, showily, galvanized; he has successes, notorieties, children, but to himself, in the situation, he is extinct. He meets the first woman again—and the dead part of him lives again. [N, p. 144]

Though never used in this form, the fable underlies two subsequent tales of literary life. In "The Death of the Lion"

(1894, in the *Yellow Book*), a writer willingly and fatally offers himself to a lionizing hostess while his literary critic friend marries a young woman who shares the critic's love for the artist's work. The artist is not saved, but his work lives on in the lovers who care. In "The Next Time," a story planned and written shortly after the opening of *Guy Domville* (and published in the *Yellow Book*), the writer's situation is reversed: he cannot win a lionizing public no matter how hard he tries.[31] Only when he accepts the nature of his talent does he gain "a greater freedom with his wife" (XV, 211) and with this the confidence that permits him "a grand indifference...a reckless consciousness of art" in which "The voice of the market had suddenly grown faint and far" (XV, 215).

But even when the minority writer explicitly acknowledged his role, as James did in publishing in little magazines like the *Chap-Book* or the *Yellow Book,* the "voice of the market," or at least of a segment of it, was never completely still. Max Beerbohm, in writing of literary life in the nineties in "Enoch Soames," spoke of "the *mot juste,* that Holy Grail of the period."[32] Love for the *mot juste* that reflects *fin de siècle* world-weariness inspires the title of Soame's first—and wretched—book, *Negations.* In real life, it inspired the little magazine authors. Frederick Wedmore of the *Savoy* published *Renunciations* in 1893, while from the *Yellow Book* authors there came Herbert Crackanthorpe's *Wreckage* in 1893, George Egerton's (Mary Chavelita Bright) *Keynotes* in 1893 and *Discords* in 1894, Ella D'Arcy's *Monochromes* in 1895, Ernest Dowson's *Dilemmas* in 1895—and Henry James's *Terminations* and *Embarrassments.* Retreat to the purely private is never possible for the author who would publish. For all his "grand indifference," even the artist in "The Next Time" hears the faint "voice of the market"; his last book is called "Derogation."

For a writer as alert to the concerns of his culture as

James was, discovery and acceptance of his place as a minority writer did not lessen his interest in the larger literary marketplace. Despite their personal relevance, the tales of literary life are part of a distinct mode of the nineties to which both minority and popular writers contributed. James's stories are one in spirit with Vernon Lee's *Miss Brown,* in which a painter violates his standards to paint "blazing sunsets and green moonlights"[33] because such things enable him to support his family—and then warns his friend not to follow his example; George Gissing's *New Grub Street,* in which the protagonist also turns against his better instincts to court the marketplace in order to support his family but destroys himself morally and physically instead; and Rudyard Kipling's best seller, *The Light that Failed* (1891), in which the love of friends prevents the hero from yielding to the same instincts that destroy Gissing's character.[34] And they are related by opposition to Grant Allen's "The Pot Boiler" (1892), a story about an artist who is tempted to paint "aesthetic" pictures until his child falls ill. He returns to painting salable domestic scenes, explaining to a friend, "I've yielded to Duty.... It may be heroic to despise comfort and fame and wealth and security for the sake of high art and the best that's in one. I dare say it is; but I'm sure it's a long way more heroic still to do work one doesn't want to do for wife and children."[35] Given James's willingness to cast even his personal problems in a popular mode, it is not surprising that when he returned to the novel in the late nineties, he did not withdraw "into a dreamy interior world" or devote himself to abstract "experiments in form." Instead, he continued to write with an eye to the best sellers of the period, still working within and against popular conventions. If his hope of winning a broad following was gone, his desire to leave a compelling picture of his time was as alive as ever.

SIX

What Maisie Knew

With the publication of *What Maisie Knew,* James made it clear to the world that he was returning to the novel.[1] He had eased himself back into the genre with the conversion of his play scenario for *The Other House* and with *The Spoils of Poynton,* a novella or perhaps long short story which lacks the breadth and density we associate with the novel. Even *Maisie* seems narrower in compass than the novels of the eighties. James's concern with the ills of upper-class London life and his adoption of the child's point of view are such restrictions of scope that it has been easy for critics to emphasize James's emotional withdrawal from the wider life around him and his formal experimentation in the novel. Viewed in the context of the book's slow conception and its publication, however, such critical emphases are only partially acceptable. Both James's choice of material—the experience of the child and the nature of upper-class London life—and his use of the child's point of view reveal his continuing interest in the themes and formal elements of popular and best-selling fiction as well as contemporary drama. In this context, the novel appears less narrow and less personal than we have thought. As in the eighties, but now with no illusions of acceptance by the mass market, James exploits popular literary conventions to provide an effective critique of his society and its assumptions about itself.

Maisie took shape gradually in James's mind. The first notebook entry on the work is dated November 1892. James records a dinner-table anecdote about a child consigned by the court to spend equal amounts of time in the custody of each of her divorced parents. He sees a tale in this and starts adding ideas: the child's parents could remarry and lose interest in the child, while the stepparents take over the abdicated parental roles and form a relationship between themselves through the child. The child's situation is further clarified in a second note of August 1893 in which James suggests that the child's parents leave their second spouses, literally abandoning the child to her stepparents. A third notebook entry in December 1895 shows James beginning to work on the novel, though at this point he is still thinking of it as a tale. In this entry he locates his point of view in the child's perception of events and outlines the work as a whole, adding now the idea that the parents form new liaisons after they leave the stepparents and introducing an additional character who is eventually to bring up the child herself. In subsequent notebook entries James acknowledges that the tale has grown into a novel and works out further details of the plot. But the first three entries are of special interest because they show us the major additions James made to the original anecdote: first, the almost mechanical proliferation of liaisons among the adults (an addition that gives the novel its pronounced symmetry and in the process serves to dehumanize the characters involved), and second, the focus on the sensitive outcast child (an addition that gives James an extraordinary central consciousness and so creates the pathos—and as James argues in his preface to the New York Edition, the beauty [XI, xi–xii]—of the novel).

We can account in good part for the expansion of James's original anecdote by looking at other literature of the early nineties. As divorce became increasingly public and increasingly acceptable, it also became subject matter for the popular writer. Divorce novels began appearing in America in the eighties and in England in the nineties, as Howells's *A Modern Instance* (1882) and Hardy's *Jude the Obscure* (1896) remind us. Particularly relevant to James's novel is the fact that between 1892 and 1895, the years in which *Maisie* was taking shape and James was most attentive to the English stage, every major English playwright was writing "problem plays" about the Marriage Question—and usually doing so in sensational terms, adultery being more interesting and less confusing morally to audiences than other aspects of the question. The Marriage Question play was extremely popular; it was topical, titillating, often amusing, and always moral.[2] These plays appeared in rapid succession: Oscar Wilde's *Lady Windermere's Fan* (1892) and *A Woman of No Importance* (1893), Arthur Wing Pinero's *The Second Mrs. Tanqueray* (1893), *The Notorious Mrs. Ebbsmith* (1895), and *The Benefit of the Doubt* (1895), and Henry Arthur Jones's *The Case of Rebellious Susan* (1894) and *The Masqueraders* (1894). We know James saw some of these plays; given his interest in the theater, we can assume he saw most if not all of the others.[3]

In their handling of marital discord, these plays bear a closer resemblance to *Maisie* than do such novels as Howells's or Hardy's. Like *Maisie* they deal with upper-class English life where infidelity is a response to the boredom of the wealthy; liaisons are formed easily and frequently, creating in some instances farcelike episodes where characters find out or barely miss finding out who has been sleeping with whom; and the grossest immoralities, of course, take place on the other side of the Channel. It is probable that

James had popular drama in mind when writing *Maisie*.[4] He had dealt with easy contemporary morals in his London fiction before the Marriage Question play became popular—in "The Siege of London" (1882), "The Path of Duty" (1885), "A London Life" (1889), and "The Chaperon" (1891). But in none of these stories is there the on-stage proliferation of partners and the comic orchestration of meetings between lovers and ex-lovers that there is in *Maisie*. And James was certainly conscious of the theatrical quality of his novel. *Maisie* was the second book (*Poynton* was the first) for which he wrote a scenario; and in his notebook, he exhorted himself, "the *scenic* method is my absolute, my imperative, my *only* salvation" (*N*, p. 263).

Divorce, however, is only the background of *Maisie;* the history of a child is the foreground and greater part of the novel. In developing his original anecdote so that the central concern of the novel is the child's sensibilities, James further shows himself to be one with his cultural situation. This has not been recognized by those critics who, in accounting for the content of the book, have stressed its personal relevance for James. Edmund Wilson and Leon Edel offer extreme examples of this approach. For Wilson, Maisie is one of many little girls in James's fiction whom James equated with his own vulnerability and whom he wished to destroy in the dark period after his failure as a playwright.[5] For Edel, Maisie is one of several children in James's fiction through whom he vicariously grew up and regained self-confidence after his difficulties in the theater.[6] But if the preoccupation with a helpless child-protagonist is neurotic—and to our sensibilities it certainly seems so in some degree—it was a neurosis that James shared with his age. A sense of helplessness in the face of widespread social change was common. James's inability to find a receptive audience for his novels and his plays was only one version of the common plight.

In response to this feeling of helplessness, many writers in the nineties indulged themselves in an imagined return to the apparent simplicity of childhood—and readers responded appreciatively. So prevalent were books about children that *Scribner's,* which had serialized several of these books, commented in April 1896 on the existence of "a new child literature": "The child's mind and his world are really new literary themes—almost the only elementary phases of life, when you think of it, that it has been left to our time to take up; and their literature is in a kind of Elizabethan age."[7] Max Beerbohm noted a parallel between popular fiction and a contemporary enthusiasm for children, which he cynically described as a "jaded longing for simplicity" following a surfeit of such "bizarre fashions" as slumming and aestheticism. "[N]ow that children are booming, the publishers and reviewers are all agog,"[8] he observed, and Herbert S. Stone, the publisher of *Maisie,* bore out his point in advertisements of James's novel, which noted, "It is especially interesting as being Mr. James's first study of child-life."[9] In evaluating James's achievement in *Maisie,* then, we may acknowledge a neurotic component in the novel, but we must also recognize the novel as a deliberate contribution to a particular literary and social context. Viewed in this light, it is evident that James fought against the regressive tendencies of his genre even while he indulged himself in it.

Oscar Cargill is the only critic who suggests that James "read up" on childhood in preparation for writing *Maisie.*[10] Some of the titles he offers, however, present problems. For example, he notes James's familiarity with Eliot's *The Mill on the Floss* (1860) and *Silas Marner* (1861) and with Daudet's *Le Petit Chose* (1868) and *Jack* (1876). But there is no evidence that James read these books immediately prior to writing *Maisie,* and to observe that he had read them at some point is merely to observe that he had read the same books many other nineteenth-century readers had read. A related problem arises with Edmond de Goncourt's *Chérie* (1883). Cargill recalls James's discussion of the book in "The Art of Fiction." He cites James's then expressed conviction that "the development of the moral consciousness of a child" is a fit subject for fiction and his disappointment in Goncourt's handling of the subject. From this, Cargill concludes, "A determination formed to improve upon the study made by Edmond"—a determination that resulted first in "The Pupil" (1891) and then in *Maisie*. As we have seen in the case of *The Tragic Muse*, James sometimes did think in terms of redoing what he felt others had done badly. But a substantial period of time intervened between *Chérie* and *Maisie*, and we have no way of knowing whether *Chérie* or the issue it raised remained with James all those years. Although Cargill's suggestion in regard to this source is plausible, we must accept it with caution.

I think Cargill is on firmer ground when he looks at material that we know James encountered closer to the actual writing of his novel. But he has disappointingly few suggestions to offer. A reference in *Maisie* to Mrs. Micawber leads him to suggest that James looked at *David Copperfield* "when he was studying the terrors of childhood," but he traces the influence no further. The circumstances surrounding the children in both *Copperfield* and *Maisie* are different enough so that, although we cannot deny Dickens's influence, we must say that it is rather general—as perhaps Cargill's brevity on the subject confesses—and that there is equal justification for seeing it behind James's concept of the child's character as well as in the terrors surrounding childhood. A second suggestion is rather timidly put forth: the denouement of James's novel, Cargill offers, was "unconsciously influenced" by Marcel Prévost's *Lettres de femmes* (1892–94), that is, James was writing in reaction to Prévost. Citing this influence is as far as Cargill goes in describing the contemporary context of *Maisie*. But the popular context I have alluded to also impinged on *Maisie,* and Cargill's main point, that James's novel is indebted to other fiction, can be argued more convincingly than he does.

Stevenson had prepared the way for the outpouring of child literature in the nineties with his fiction and poetry in the preceding decade. In his essay on Stevenson (in the *Century,* April 1888), James commented favorably on the two qualities in his work that were to recur in the later child literature: its evocation of the child's perspective and its foundation in memory.[11] James undoubtedly knew some of the child literature that followed as well. Many of these books went even further than Stevenson in providing an escape from the present by indulgently examining the world created by the child protagonist's imagination. There are Kenneth Grahame's two books, *The Golden Age* (1895) and *Dream Days* (1898), which appeared first in the form of individual sketches in the *New Review,* the *Yellow Book,* and the *Chap-Book* in the mid-nineties, when James was publishing in those magazines, and were widely and enthusiastically reviewed when published in book form. Less popular, but probably also known to James, was a work by his friend Frances Hodgson Burnett, a book whose full title is *The One I Knew Best of All: A Memory of the Mind of a Child.* This was one of the novels that *Scribner's* serialized (January to June, 1893)—one installment appearing in an issue (May) that also included James's "The Middle Years." Another of *Scribner's* serializations was James M. Barrie's best-selling *Sentimental Tommy: The Story of His Boyhood* (January to November, 1896), a book that James probably knew of whether he read it or not, since he was acquainted with Barrie at the time and since the cult of Barrie was well established years before the publication of *Peter Pan* (1902, as *The Little White Bird*). A final example of the genre is Margaret Deland's *The Story of a Child.* This book was serialized in the *Atlantic* (September to November, 1892) and attracted some attention, not for its intrinsic merits, which are few, but because Deland had earlier written the popular *John Ward, Preacher* (1887).[12]

The work of Dickens, Eliot, and Twain lies generally behind the child literature of the nineties. We consequently find children who are harassed and misunderstood by adults and children who are sentimentalized as redemptive figures. But the child literature of the nineties differs markedly from its predecessors. While earlier writers treat childhood as a time of preparation for adulthood and consequently write for an audience that includes children, the end-of-the-century writers treat childhood as a time of evasion of mature responsibility and address themselves to an audience of other discontented adults. The books of these writers are based on reminiscence: in some more or less disguised manner, each author recollects his own childhood and locates his novel in the now vanished world of his youth (in the case of *Sentimental Tommy,* it is the world of Barrie's mother's youth). But his motive is not that of the historian: nowhere in these books do we find the detailed rendering of external reality that characterizes earlier child literature, and that in the case of American child fiction reflected a desire to preserve, or better, recreate, a world that had been destroyed by the Civil War. Instead, the writer of the nineties seeks occasion for self-indulgent nostalgia. The appeal of such fiction to the adult reader was acutely summarized in a column in *Scribner's* in January 1898: "Little by little...widespread awakening of intelligent interest in childhood is finding expression in literature. In the wastes of tawdry 'realism,' iconoclasm, cynicism, and shamelessness, men have lifted up voices of regret for the epic age [of childhood], and cried aloud for the times when life was simpler."[13]

Like the child protagonists of earlier fiction, the protagonists of the nineties novels are orphaned or semiorphaned and in consequence misunderstood or unappreciated. But it is the quality of the child's mind, not the quality of his life, that most concerns the writer of the nineties. Tommy's epithet, "sentimental," is particularly applicable to each of the children of the nineties, and their fantasies and games— obvious responses to loneliness—form the major part of each novel. Burnett's subtitle, *A Memory of the Mind of a Child,* in fact, could be appended to each of these novels. Barrie and Deland describe the perceptions and fantasies of a child from an omniscient point of view. But Burnett and Grahame approach the subject with greater skill and tact. While using the language of an adult and speaking occasionally from the perspective of an adult, both writers recapture the limited vision of the child by adopting a child's point of view. Burnett's *The One I Knew Best of All* is an autobiographical account of her own childhood and her discovery of her storytelling abilities. She narrates the story in the third person, coyly referring to herself as "the Small Person" but nevertheless delicately and convincingly conveying the changing thoughts and perceptions of a growing child. Grahame's books, *The Golden Age* and *Dream Days,* are less closely autobiographical, though they are rooted in the general circumstances of Grahame's childhood (he was raised with brothers and a sister by relatives). Grahame's narrator is the middle child of a group of five; he tells his stories in the first person, conveying only what he or occasionally one of his fictional siblings might have thought and known.

Unlike most earlier child novels, these novels of the nineties (with the exception of Burnett's) are not stories of psychological and social growth. In earlier novels, when imaginative protagonists appear, their play is purposeful. The children in *Little Women* (1868, 1869) and *Tom Sawyer* (1876), for example, play games based on the fiction they have read. The play is an escape from the dullness and

spiritual poverty of small town life, but it also is a preparation for adulthood. The girls in *Little Women* play at romances that end in marriages of true love and material
comfort; the boys in *Tom Sawyer* play games of conquest that
have as their prizes fabulous wealth and beautiful women.
And the fantasies, having taught the children appropriate
social roles and values, are fulfilled in the conclusions of the
novels. In the novels of the nineties, by contrast, play serves
only the purpose of escape. The children in these novels,
like the children in the earlier books, are profoundly impressed by the fiction they have read. But their games of
conquest are invariably foiled, their romances never
brought to fruition. Burnett's heroine tells stories that have
no ending. Deland's heroine dreams of death, martyrdom,
and escape when, as repeatedly happens, she finds herself
at odds with her strict grandmother whom she loves but
with whom she cannot communicate. Grahame's fictional
children frequently find refuge from the insensitivities of
their guardians—aunts and uncles, not parents—by creating imaginary cities in which all wishes are gratified. In no
way do such fantasies prepare the child—or the reader who
identifies with the child—for the accommodation to social
reality that we define as maturity.

The anecdote that inspired *Maisie* imposed some constraints on the direction James's story would take, for the
anecdote gave him contemporary London life as a setting
and an abandoned child as a central character. Still, there
was room to maneuver: the background, for example,
might have been minimized and the story allowed to become the escapist fantasy that other child literature was.
Instead, James developed both background and foreground, incorporating in his book the concerns of both
popular drama and child literature. The result is a novel in
which contemporary adult life with its breakdown of sexual
mores is examined. The child novel, a genre of evasion in

the nineties, in James's hands becomes one of confrontation.

For most critics, James's handling of the point of view
which governs this novel is admirable, for the adult narrator
convincingly conveys what is perceived by a growing child
who frequently sees more than she can understand. The
novel is seen as a continuation of James's earlier experiments with a restricted point of view and, because of the
extreme limitations of the child's knowledge, as a technical
challenge that James created for himself and met magnificently. Occasionally James has been criticized for writing a
novel in which the viewpoint is uncomfortably voyeuristic
and immature: in reading the novel, we are forced to iden-
tify with the child who watches and speculates on the inti-
macies of the adults around her.[14] Consideration of James's
literary context requires us to temper both critical responses. James's handling of the child's point of view is
remarkable for its care and sensitivity, but not for its
uniqueness. James had Burnett and Grahame as models; in
writing from Maisie's point of view, he was simply making
his child novel conform to other examples of the genre. But
unlike James, neither Burnett nor Grahame forces the child
protagonist to confront the adult world. It is because
James's does this that his book is open to the charge of
being voyeuristic. Yet contemporary critics never complained about this aspect of the novel.[15] The perspective was
too familiar to the nineteenth-century reader to seem unhealthy or immature. James's original readers would have
come to the novel after having read what are to our sensibilities surprisingly detailed newspaper accounts of recent
divorce trials and after having seen the numerous Marriage
Question plays where they, as members of the audience,
watched and speculated on someone else's behavior in
much the same fashion that James's Maisie does. By our
standards perhaps the perspective of *Maisie* must be termed

voyeuristic, but we must also recognize that the nineteenth-century reader would not share our uneasiness about this aspect of the novel.

The anecdote with which James began hinted at a child unloved and ultimately unwanted. As James developed Maisie's story, probably with an eye to the other child novels of the nineties, he emphasized this aspect of the story in such a way as to paint a chilling picture of upper-class London life. Throughout the novel Maisie apprehensively watches her parents and stepparents change partners and take new lovers. She understands nothing of sex at first, but she does understand self-centeredness, and she foresees that a time will come when "with two fathers, two mothers and two homes, six protections in all, she should n't know 'wherever' to go" (XI, 99). Her childhood, in fact, becomes a constant giving of herself to her elders in the hope that she will be spared the fate she fears. But her hope and trust are ultimately to no avail. Her parents, Beale and Ida Farange, both brutally and finally reject her so that they will be free of domestic responsibilities. Her stepmother, Mrs. Beale, regards her as a rival for the attentions of her stepfather, Sir Claude, and turns viciously against the child. Sir Claude, who does care for Maisie and whom Maisie adores, is finally too weak to give up Mrs. Beale and become a proper father to the child. And at the end of the novel, Maisie is left in the hands of her governess, Mrs. Wix, who has the virtue of loving the girl but the vice of a narrow and dirty mind. In short, the divorce settlement itself and the easy morals of upper-class London life as effectively orphan Maisie as the deaths of parents orphan her literary peers.

In portraying the unstable lives of Maisie's parents and stepparents as he did, James was following out an idea that he first explored in "A London Life": that male and female sexuality are essentially the same, that the time-honored double standard and, by implication, the social order based on it cannot be considered natural. The idea was certainly not a new one for the period, but it was not a popular one either. I have suggested that the farcelike manipulation of lovers in *Maisie* owes something to the popular Marriage Question plays; but the morality of the novel owes nothing to this source and perhaps represents a deliberate violation of popular assumptions, a violation made all the more striking for being clothed in a familiar form. The Marriage Question plays seemed daring when they were first produced because they openly admitted the existence of female sexuality. But the admission was greatly qualified. The double standard was accepted as natural; an erring woman's behavior was made palatable, sometimes justifiable, by an inconsiderate husband and an understanding lover. And if the woman had a child, she inevitably appealed to the audience's sympathy by offering to forgo her own happiness— in the context of these plays, gratification of her sexual desires—for the sake of her child. Wilde's Lady Windermere is deterred by her own repentant, self-sacrificing mother from running away from her husband by the words, "[E]ven if he [your husband] had a thousand loves, you must stay with your child. If he was harsh to you, you must stay with your child. If he ill-treated you, you must stay with your child. If he abandoned you, your place is with your child" (act 3). Her decision to stay home for the sake of her child is repeated over and over again in the Marriage Question plays. What Wilde and the other playwrights have done, in short, is to acknowledge female sexuality but insist at the same time that it is naturally guided and checked by affection and maternal instinct. James, by denying the naturalness of the double standard, denies the efficacy of such checks. For him, there is nothing innate in women—or in men, for that matter—that will, without external support, provide for the survival of the family. And in a novel whose world is characterized initially by a divorce-court settlement that consigns a child to spend equal amounts of time with two unfit parents, there is little in the way of external support.

Such a setting robs Maisie Farange of the resource of imaginative escape that is available to her fictional peers when feelings of loneliness, betrayal, or rejection become unbearable. For them, there is a known world against which to construct an imagined escape. For Maisie, reality is at best incomprehensible, at worst terrifying. Consequently the images through which James conveys Maisie's vision of life reverberate with the suggestion of more than a neglected child's bewilderment. The last time she sees her mother, for example, she ventures to recall the Captain and his kind words. Ida is enraged at her daughter's partiality for her former lover, and she turns angrily on the child. Maisie reacts: "there rose in her a fear, a pain, a vision ominous, precocious, of what it might mean for her mother's fate to have forfeited such a loyalty as that. There was literally an instant in which Maisie fully saw—saw madness and desolation, saw ruin and darkness and death" (XI, 225). Maisie's vision is not, as we might reasonably expect from a child instinctively drawn to another abandoned soul, a glimpse of the loneliness and boredom that will be the probable outcome of Ida's life; rather, it is an apprehension of the spiritual death manifest in such a life. This glimpse of the darkness and chaos behind the visible surface of life recalls Hyacinth Robinson's vision of a world poised unknowingly on the brink of destruction—a vision with which James sympathized. Here, too, the character's vision is enhanced by the author's, for the presentiment of spiritual death, though not inappropriate to Maisie's feelings, is the product of an adult mind and is clearly beyond her conception. Elsewhere James's presence is felt too: when he describes Maisie's vision of life in images more suited to her juvenile state, he does not suggest a coherent world that she

is too young to understand, but rather he blurs her vision
with his own to suggest a world that is at its heart fright-
eningly unstable.[16]

In one set of recurring images, Maisie sees herself and is
seen as being like a character in a story whose plot she
cannot understand. After describing the divorce settlement
that divides Maisie between her parents, James observes,
"Only a drummer-boy in a ballad or a story could have been
so in the thick of the fight. She was taken into the confidence of passions on which she fixed just the stare she
might have had for images bounding across the wall in the
slide of a magic-lantern" (XI, 9). Later, when Maisie is taken
by her father to the home of his rich mistress, the brown
American "countess," James notes, "The child had been in
thousands of stories—all Miss Wix's and her own, to say
nothing of the richest romances of French Elise—but she
had never been in such a story as this" (XI, 175). The stuff
of imagination for Maisie's literary counterparts is the stuff
of reality for her. Consequently, the kind of fiction that
provides the basis for their daydreaming and playacting
provides a gloss on existence as good as anything else
available for Maisie. Mrs. Wix, who is pitifully ignorant of
every standard subject a governess should know, "took
refuge [from her ignorance] on the firm ground of fiction,
through which indeed there curled the blue river of truth.
She knew swarms of stories, mostly those of the novels she
had read; relating them with a memory that never faltered
and a wealth of detail that was Maisie's delight. They were
all about love and beauty and countesses and wickedness"
(XI, 27)—which is to say, they were all about Maisie's elders.

Alternatively, Maisie is like a player in a game whose rules
she does not know, for unlike the games in other child
novels, this is one made up by the adults. As a small child,
"she found in her mind a collection of images and echoes to
which meanings were attachable—images and echoes kept

for her in the childish dusk, the dim closet, the high drawers, like games she was n't yet big enough to play" (XI, 12). The elaborate board games with incomprehensible directions that Sir Claude brings Maisie are emblematic of her position in life. Maisie's parents play billiards—a game which with its cues and balls is clearly a symbolic shorthand for the sexual games they play. And indeed, their sexual behavior like the behavior of Maisie's stepparents is described repeatedly by the narrator and by the adults in the novel as a "game." Maisie's initial consideration of her position in the midst of this game leads her to analogies with other games with which she is familiar—but significantly, they are games whose central feature is chaotic movement. Reflection on the unstable alliances among her parents and guardians leads her to a mental drawing up of sides and to the further reflection that "It sounded...very much like puss-in-the-corner, and she could only wonder if the distribution of parties would lead to a rushing to and fro and changing of places. She was in the presence, she felt, of restless change..." (XI, 95). When Mrs. Wix urges Sir Claude to make a home with herself—and Maisie, of course—Maisie reflects on the role she plays in other people's lives: "the sharpened sense of spectatorship was the child's main support, the long habit, from the first, of seeing herself in discussion and finding in the fury of it— she had had a glimpse of the game of football—a sort of compensation for the doom of a peculiar passivity" (XI, 107).

Such a reality is fabulous; it is perplexing; it numbs the imagination while it provokes the mind. And Maisie, who is as perceptive and sensitive as her literary peers, is finally unlike them, for she is not an imaginative child. By not basing Maisie's life on his own as other contemporary novelists did with their child protagonists, James was freed from the temptation to make her an artist in embryo. Burnett's very different heroine, the Small Person, in many ways typifies the protagonist of the child novel. She invites particular comparison with Maisie because James very likely knew her and had her in mind when creating Maisie. While the Small Person "happened to be born, as a clever but revoltingly candid and practical medical man once told her, with a cerebral tumor of the Imagination,"[17] Maisie was "to see much more than she at first understood, but also even at first to understand much more than any little girl, however patient, had perhaps ever understood before" (XI, 9), and ultimately, "As she was condemned to know more and more, how could it logically stop before she knew Most?" (XI, 281). Imagination is the Small Person's province, knowledge Maisie's.

The nature of Maisie's knowledge, like her unimaginative character, is determined by her environment. As a small child she quickly learns discretion. Bearing tales provokes anger; asking questions provokes derision; silence alone is conducive to peace if not real harmony. As she grows, Maisie looks increasingly for patterns in the lives around her, for rules that will explain the chaotic game in which she finds herself. J. A. Ward's approach to *Maisie* places a special emphasis on the child's "search for form." He describes her growing preoccupation with pattern and symmetry and notes her conclusion that people belong in pairs, that she cannot therefore accept life with Sir Claude and Mrs. Beale at the end of the novel for to do so would make her a part of an unworkable trio. Ward cautions, "I do not mean to suggest that Maisie's aesthetic sense alone accounts for what she knows and how she judges," but nevertheless concludes, "most of Maisie's judgments are rooted in an idea of form. These formal judgments represent a kind of improvised morality, perhaps all that one in Maisie's circumstances can be expected to achieve."[18] Ward is certainly correct in emphasizing Maisie's aesthetic sensibilities, her thirst for "rules" to describe her experience, and her freedom from conventional morality. At the same time, his approach—which I find genuinely illuminating and a necessary corrective to those critics who deal with Maisie's morality or lack of it[19]—leads him to underrate Maisie's psychological growth. Perhaps his sense of caution betrays a recognition of this. At all events, a final component in Maisie's growth is her discovery of her own sexuality and with this, her sympathetic appraisal of the adults around her. It is this sympathy that permits *Maisie* a final critical evaluation of society lacking in other child novels.

James carefully documents Maisie's growing sexual awareness. As a small child, she perceives that men treat her differently from the way women do. Their joking and teasing, which we recognize as covert flirting, contrast sharply with the false sympathy and overt hostility of women, who see in the child a potential rival for male attention. Her perception of this, and her consequent preference for male attention, is the beginning of sexual self-awareness. Increased powers of perception and heightened emotional capacity come with adolescence, and with this change, Maisie obtains the central clue to adult behavior. If she does not know literally what lovers do together—and there is no evidence that she does[20]—she does know how lovers feel toward each other, and that is enough.

Maisie's trip with Sir Claude when she is about thirteen, first to Folkestone and then across the Channel to Boulogne, objectifies the change that comes with adolescence. Perhaps James was acting on a hint from Burnett, for her Small Person moves from Manchester, England, to a wooded area in Tennessee at the same point in her life as Maisie goes to France. In both cases, the change of scene provides an outlet for the growing assertiveness and heightened powers of perception that come with new-found sexuality. The Small Person "began to deal with emotions. She

found emotions interesting—and forests and Autumn
leaves assisted them and seemed a part of them somehow, as
she was a part of the forests themselves."[21] For Maisie, "On
the spot, at Boulogne, though there might have been excess
there was at least no wavering; she recognised, she understood, she adored and took possession; feeling herself attuned to everything and laying her hand, right and left, on
what had simply been waiting for her" (XI, 232). Such maturity enables the imaginative Small Person to write better
stories than she did as a child; it enables Maisie to bring a
new perspective to the storylike world around her. While
she is still somewhat dependent on Mrs. Wix and her fic-
tion-based formulas—the "moral sense" that Mrs. Wix cites
so frequently and that Maisie unsuccessfully tries to com-
prehend is clearly an expression of the moralistic sensibilities that feed on romantic fiction—Maisie's new-found
sexuality does give her another key to reality to use along-
side that supplied by Mrs. Wix in the last third of the novel.

As the book approaches its conclusion, Maisie and Sir
Claude spend a last morning together. Sir Claude has resumed relations with Mrs. Beale, and from Mrs. Wix's point
of view, proved himself "a poor sunk slave...To his passions"
(XI, 313). But Maisie, who has begun to understand sexual
desire and who has always loved Sir Claude, judges him
differently. Her new maturity allows her to recognize her
mother at Folkestone and Mrs. Beale at Boulogne as allur-
ing women. Recognizing this and judging by her own feelings for Sir Claude, she can emphathize with him and so
judge him from a perspective that is both realistic and
compassionate. As a younger child, she fought against her
own intimations of weakness on Sir Claude's part. Now she
understands that he cannot help his enthrallment to
women, that he is victimized by his own nature: "Why was
such a man so often afraid? It must have begun to come to

her *now* that there was one thing just such a man above all could be afraid of. He could be afraid of himself. His fear at all events was there; his fear was sweet to her, beautiful and tender to her..." (XI, 326; my italics). Mrs. Wix's formulas require either approval or condemnation; they do not allow, as Maisie's more mature knowledge does, for a love that accepts weakness. When Sir Claude asks Maisie to live with Mrs. Beale and himself, she responds by asking him to give up Mrs. Beale, sensing even as she asks that he cannot. In her newfound maturity, she understands that Mrs. Beale would be a rival for Sir Claude's attention and she wants him to herself—though we need not assume that she is quite literally propositioning her stepfather. When he fails her, she steadfastly refuses to join Mrs. Wix in her condemnation of the couple and repeats only, "I love Sir Claude—I love *him*" (XI, 359).

Instead of turning from an inhospitable everyday world to the self-gratifying realm of the imagination, Maisie has gone from a storybook world to one in which authentic emotion and compassion operate. Her history thus reverses that of the typical child novel protagonist. But more than a simple reversal of convention is involved in this novel. The storybook world that Maisie transcends, as I said earlier, is the contemporary social world as James sees it, and Mrs. Wix, with all her rigidity, expresses the code of values that society pays lip service to if nothing more. James's depiction of Maisie's growth is his implicit condemnation of such a society. Yet because the storybook world is the real one, there is no escape for Maisie as there is for the other child protagonists of the nineties. The last events of James's novel embody his—and Maisie's—recognition of this fact. When Maisie discovers that she cannot have Sir Claude on her own terms, she accepts life with Mrs. Wix. Her rejection of Sir Claude's proposal that she live with Mrs. Beale and himself, even as she loves him, and her acceptance of Mrs. Wix, even as she has begun to recognize the governess's limitations, are mature acts. Maisie's behavior reflects an informed, sensitive evaluation of her position in relation to the adults around her. As such, it is an accommodation to reality found nowhere else in the child literature of the nineties.

SEVEN

The Awkward Age

In a New York Edition preface nearly as inadequate as the preface to *The Tragic Muse,* James presents *The Awkward Age* as a novel that started from a humble impetus and emerged as a significant technical success. He began, he tells us, with an interest in "minor 'social phenomena'" (IX, vi), the crises produced in English households when a daughter can no longer be relegated to the schoolroom but is considered too immature because of her unmarried state to be admitted to the adult conversation downstairs. As a theme, "It was not," he continues belittlingly, "a fine purple peach, but it might pass for a round ripe plum" (IX, vi). The *roman dialogué* practiced in the eighties and nineties by the popular French writer "Gyp" (Sibylle Gabrielle Marie Antoinette de Riquette de Mirabeau, Countess de Martel de Janville) and her follower Henri Lavedan struck him as the ideal form for such a light work—but with the text type set to look like a conventional novel, which James deemed more attractive to the English reader than the French playbook form. The resulting novel, however, greatly exceeded James's expectations. It grew to an extraordinary length according to some principle of which he professed absolute incomprehension, and it outgrew its initial association with "Gyp" to become more dense and complex than her work and at the same

time much tighter in construction. Looking back at the
novel, James concluded, "The thing carries itself to my ma-
turer and gratified sense as with every symptom of sound-
ness, an insolence of health and joy" (IX, xxiii)—and he felt
this in spite of the fact that the reception of the book had
provoked his publisher to remark, "I've never in all my experience seen one [a book] treated with more general and
complete disrespect" (IX, xv).

We have no reason to doubt James's satisfaction with the
novel. But his account of the novel's origins is suspect. Examination of the book in its literary context reveals James's
indebtedness to two enthusiasms of the nineties: the English dialogue novel and the New Woman novel. This background in turn accounts for the amplitude of James's book:
both the dialogue novel and the New Woman novel were
associated with issues larger than the "minor 'social phenomena'" that James began with; when added to his germ,
they transfigured it. This is another of the many cases in
which James's friends worked in the genres that he too
tried, and did so with considerably more popular success
than he had. We can assume that as in other cases, his sense
of dignity governed his silence on the popular context of his
work. But such silence has had the unfortunate effect of
diminishing James's novel. Although modern critics have
occasionally observed that *The Awkward Age* presents a
richer picture of contemporary British life than James's
preface suggests, his silence has permitted many to read this
book, like *Maisie*, simply as a technical experiment—in this
case overstressing James's indebtedness to the drama with
its scenes and dialogue—or as an event in James's psychological history.[1]

The dialogue novel in English probably owes its initial
impetus to "Gyp," although her novels were not available in
translation until the mid-nineties and the form had appeared earlier in England. *Punch* ran occasional dialogues

through the eighties and published a regular series called "Voces Populi" starting in 1888, while *Black and White* began a series called "The World We Live In" in 1892.[2] These series dialogues were short, unrelated or loosely related dramatizations of amusing social difficulties, prose cartoons in effect. The form was soon picked up by other newspapers and weeklies in both America and England, and the notion that witty dialogue was somehow appropriate to popular journalism may account for the willingness with which *Harper's Weekly* agreed to run *The Awkward Age*.[3] Once a popular taste for the form was evident, books in dialogue also began appearing—sometimes set up like playbooks, sometimes looking like conventional novels, and sometimes combining both forms. The public was eager for the genre no matter what it looked like.[4]

We know James read one English dialogue novel and can reasonably assume he saw others. In 1893, his friend E. F. Benson published *Dodo: A Detail of the Day*, a novel that attracted wide attention because it was generally understood to be a roman à clef fictionalizing Margot Tennant's witty and articulate social circle, the "Souls." Although James was not a member of the group, he could claim acquaintance with its members, and this circumstance alone probably would have prompted his interest in the book.[5] But we need not speculate, for James did read an early version of this book and reacted by commenting "delicately" on it: in one of his autobiographies, Benson notes James's response as being a "wisely expressed opinion, that opinion, in fact, being no opinion at all"[6] and quotes part of a letter in which James speaks rather generally of the value of style. In addition, James probably saw the work of other friends. F. Anstey (Thomas Anstey Guthrie) was the anonymous author of *Punch's* "Voces Populi" as well as other dialogue pieces and serials for *Punch*. He published a number of collections of these dialogues in the nineties along with *Lyre and Lancet: A Story in Scenes* (1895), a novel-length work. Violet Hunt published parts of her first dialogue novel, *The Maiden's Progress: A Novel in Dialogue* (1894), in a variety of journals, including *Black and White* and the *Pall Mall Gazette.* Since James published in the former and read the latter, he probably saw some of the sketches if not the novel as a whole. Hunt was soon recognized as an accomplished writer of the genre, and her next novel, *A Hard Woman: A Story in Scenes* (1895), was extensively reviewed and advertised. There were best sellers in the genre too. *The Dolly Dialogues,* by Anthony Hope (Anthony Hope Hawkins), first published as sketches in the *Westminster Gazette,* appeared in book form in 1894 and was nearly as popular as his other book of the same year, *The Prisoner of Zenda,*[7] while Ellen Thorneycroft Fowler's *Concerning Isabel Carnaby* was a best seller in the year that James wrote and began serializing *The Awkward Age.* It is against this background, in part, that James's novel should be judged.

Two observations must be made about these popular novels. First, the dialogue form serves no real function. Its use in *Dodo* is understandable, for the book depicts a circle famous for its witty and free talk. But Benson brings no critical intelligence to bear on this fact: his fictional characters simply talk a great deal because their life models did. Benson does not ask what their conversations tell us about the society he is depicting. In the other novels, there is even less justification for the dialogue form. The characters are educated, articulate upper-class Englishmen and women, but none of the books depicts a group as tightly knit and as self-consciously intellectual as the "Souls." Instead, what we have in Anstey's, Hope's, and Hunt's books is talk for its own sake, emphasized by an extremely high percentage of dialogue in each book, chapters that are anecdotal in nature, and the use of the word "dialogue" or "scene" in the titles, calling the prospective reader's attention to the form.

Fowler's novel is more conventional: the percentage of dialogue is high but the sections of dialogue are introduced by substantial prose passages. Yet here too the talk is not functional: situations often seem to exist so that characters can have an opportunity to talk, and they talk on far longer than need be.

James, as we might expect, used the dialogue form very self-consciously. His letter to Henrietta Reubell about *The Awkward Age* implies that, like Benson, he too had the "Souls" or a similar group in mind when writing: "I had in view a certain special social (highly 'modern' and actual) London group and type and tone...clever people at least would know who, in general, and what, one meant."[8] The novel itself, however, has never been identified as a roman à clef; instead, the talkative circle represents contemporary English upper-class society in general. James opens his novel with a conversation between Mr. Longdon, a man of fifty-five who has not been in London for the past thirty years, and Vanderbank, a man of thirty-four who is a member of the circle in question. Their discussion defines modern London life, identifying "talk" (IX, 11) as the factor which distinguishes it from the life Longdon had known there in his youth. And as James brings out the uninhibited quality of the talk, he hints—even this early in the book— that social life established on such grounds necessarily entails a loss. Van speaks for the moderns: "it strikes you that right and left, probably, we keep giving each other away. Well, I dare say we do. Yes, 'come to think of it,' as they say in America, we do. But what shall I tell you? Practically we all know it and allow for it and it's as broad as it's long. What's London life after all? It's tit for tat!" Longdon "earnestly and pleadingly" asks, "Ah but what becomes of friendship?" (IX, 19–20). In the remainder of *The Awkward Age,* James answers Longdon's question by allowing London life to reveal itself through its particular kind of talk. The dialogue form thus becomes a means of examining a society critically.[9]

The second point to be made about the dialogue novels is that with some variations the story of a flirtation involving a heroine who is in the much-used word of the period, "clever," is a favored plot.[10] Benson's Dodo is the most tough-minded of the heroines. She marries for status and money, not love, and continues to flirt with the man she cares for. When the death of her husband frees her, she becomes engaged to the man she loves but makes a second socially advantageous marriage. Although the way she uses men is distasteful, she captivates those around her with her beauty, her spontaneity, and above all her audacity. With her insincerities, her concern with social status, and her sharp tongue, she prefigures Hunt's much less attractive Hard Woman. Dolly Foster, in Hope's book, is a sweeter example of the type. She too has rejected one suitor for a man of higher social status, but in her case, she seems to have acted wisely: her rejected suitor rather enjoys the role of disappointed lover. From his safe vantage point, he flirts with Dolly through the numerous dialogues in which she appears and talks of love in those in which she does not. While Dodo is brash, Dolly is more subtle, always pretending to an innocence she does not have. But her pretense is not malicious and she brings genuine delight to her friends. Isabel Carnaby is a third variation. She is not as pretty as Dolly and Dodo, but she is more intelligent and often witty. She is torn between her worldly impulses and her better self, and her struggle occupies most of Fowler's book. Ultimately her better instincts win and she marries a man who is both good and intelligent, though poor. In choosing him, she rejects a suitor whom she does not truly love but who could offer her a fine social position. She thus avoids repeating Dodo's mistake and so gratifies popular fondness for sentimentality and moral platitude.

Hunt's first heroine is particularly interesting in relation to her literary peers and to *The Awkward Age*. She is Mary Elizabeth Maskelyne, nicknamed Moderna, and as her name indicates, cast in a somewhat different mold from Dolly and Dodo. The book begins with her coming-out at eighteen and ends with her engagement at twenty-seven. In the nine intervening years, Moderna develops as something of a New Woman. She enjoys making herself attractive to men, but after a brief engagement to a straitlaced and over-protective suitor, she decides that she will remain a "bach-elor girl." She never develops any sort of feminist ideology but instead expresses her modernity by self-indulgently doing what she wants. What she wants is never really ris-qué—at its worst, it is a timorous association with a Bohe-mian crowd—but her behavior is enough to make her mother feel quite displaced by her modern child.[11] Mrs. Maskelyne, expressing a common maternal sentiment in the nineties, laments that her daughter "wants to know, she wants to gain her own experience, she doesn't care to make use of her mother's before her. A mother is only a kind of helpless Survival of the Unfittest...."[12] But at the end of the novel, Moderna behaves in the most traditional manner and decides to marry a wealthy, strong-willed, conservative En-glish lord. It is impossible to tell whether Hunt means to disparage Moderna's values, which she had treated rather sympathetically at first, or whether she is unthinkingly using a traditional romance ending.

In *The Awkward Age,* James varied the convention of the clever heroine in a significant way: she is no longer a young woman like her predecessors; instead, she is the *mother* of a young woman. Like her fictional predecessors, Mrs. Brookenham has a quick wit, ready sympathy, and a self-confidence that keep her at the center of her social circle. Her usual manner is neither as brash as Dodo's nor as sweet as Dolly's, yet she often plays at incomprehension or concil-

iation to avert a quarrel in her drawing room, and at the end
of the novel, she acts as audaciously as Dodo. She is also
similar to Moderna—but not to Moderna's mother. "[T]he
modern has always been my own note" (IX, 166), Mrs.
Brook tells her friends. And "the modern," as she interprets
it, means acting as if she were younger than her forty-one
years. This is most apparent in her relationship with her
daughter, Nanda, who has just been allowed to leave the
schoolroom and sit with the adults "downstairs." Nanda is
sixteen or eighteen—perhaps nineteen; Mrs. Brook lies
about her age. Further, Mrs. Brook tends to deny parental
responsibility for her child: "Why *should* I ask any [questions]
—when I want her life to be as much as possible like my
own?... From the moment she *is* down[stairs] the only thing
for us is to live as friends. I think it's so vulgar...not to have
the same good manners with one's children as one has with
other people. She asks *me* nothing" (XI, 177). While Mrs.
Maskelyne feels abandoned by her daughter, Mrs. Brook
has virtually abandoned hers by treating her as a friend
with whom one does not interfere. In casting his heroine as
an older woman, James has inverted the traditional relationship between mother and daughter—and the inversion
has major consequences for his novel.

As a result of her mother's denial of responsibility, Nanda
herself takes on the abdicated maternal role. With a prema-
ture gravity, she feels that at eighteen her character has
taken its final shape: "what I am I must remain. I have n't
what's called a principle of growth" (IX, 214). This sense of
maturity is reflected in Nanda's treatment of those around
her. She offers her unhappily married and somewhat slow-
witted friend Tishy Grendon the solace and direction a
mother might a child. To Mr. Longdon, who loved her
grandmother in vain, she offers both the affection that her
grandmother withheld and the instruction in the ways of
the present that a parent should offer. At one point, when

she and Longdon are solemnly reflecting on the differences between past and present, "she put out to him the tender hand she might have offered to a sick child" (IX, 231). It is a telling gesture that beautifully characterizes their relationship. And even more important, she provides her mother with the guidance Mrs. Brook will not grant her. Nanda cannot help but recognize that her presence in her mother's drawing room necessarily causes guests to watch what they say out of deference to her unmarried state. According to her mother, she thoughtfully absents herself: "She won't have a difference in my freedom. It's as if the dear thing *knew*, don't you see? what we must keep back. She wants us not to have to think. It's quite maternal!" (IX, 166). It is appropriate that Nanda resembles not her modern young mother, but rather her old-fashioned grandmother.

Like many of her fictional predecessors, Mrs. Brook's main interest is her extramarital flirtation. But James complicates her situation through his inversion of the mother-daughter relationship. Mrs. Brook has picked the nouveau riche Mr. Mitchett as the member of her circle whom she would like for Nanda's husband. But Nanda is attracted to her mother's admirer, the aristocratic and impoverished Vanderbank. When Mrs. Brook learns this—and it says something for her own state of infatuation that she must be told and cannot perceive it for herself—her first reaction is, "he'll never come to the scratch" (IX, 91). This is probably an accurate appraisal of Van. Although men of the 1890s frequently waited until their mid-thirties to marry, Van seems to be one of the numerous constitutionally cold men in James's work. His attention to his clothes and his comfortably furnished home despite his relatively tight finances suggest a finicky man whose own needs come first. His relationship with Mrs. Brook is, in spite of the jokes of their mutual friends, an innocent flirtation and not an affair. When Mr. Longdon recognizes Nanda's feelings for Van and understands that constant exposure to her mother's circle will lessen her marriageability by compromising her innocence, he proposes to Van that he, Longdon, put up a dowry for the girl. But Van still hesitates. If Mrs. Brook could simply wait in silence, she could keep Van on the terms she has always held him. But perceiving her daughter as a friend, she also recognizes her as a rival and so is too nervous to wait.

As James develops Mrs. Brook's rivalry with her daughter, he reveals the viciousness inherent in a society based on free talk and so uses a popular novel form for a new critical purpose. By casting a forty-one-year-old mother in a role conventionally held by a younger woman, James has given us a heroine whose behavior and attitudes can only be immature and inappropriate. Mrs. Brook shows her immaturity when she betrays Van's confidence and tells Mitchy, in Van's presence, that Mr. Longdon has offered to provide a dowry for her daughter. She characterizes the dowry as a bribe in order to discourage the scrupulous Vanderbank from accepting it. Her behavior recalls Van's earlier comment to Longdon that London life is "tit for tat," a process of "giving each other away." She is even more childish toward the end of the novel when her entire circle of friends gathers at Tishy Grendon's house. She is rude to everyone and at the end of the evening succeeds in forcing her daughter to admit publicly to having read a scandalous French novel. The admission is intended to make Nanda appear so worldly that Van will not take her and so endangered by her mother's circle that Mr. Longdon will adopt her. Ultimately, Mrs. Brook achieves both her objectives. But in the process she has talked too rudely, too bluntly, and too much; Van drops her as well as her daughter. Mrs. Brook is among the few heroines of dialogue novels whose flirtations end in failure. In meting out his punishment, James passes judgment on her and by implication on the society in which she had played a central role. Her defeat is James's condemnation of a society in which youth, modernity, and wit have taken the places formerly held by tradition, maturity, and wisdom.

The New Woman, as I noted in connection with *The Bostonians,* began appearing in American fiction in the eighties. By the nineties, she was a staple of both English and American fiction, appearing often as a major character and even more often as a minor one, a sop to popular tastes, like the occasional aesthete. William Dean Howells, in a "Life and Letters" essay in *Harper's Weekly* in 1895, considered reasons for her frequent appearance in fiction. He suggested her present attraction was less that she enabled the writer to describe social change than that she had become a thoroughly conventional type: "I have my doubts of the existence of the New Woman on any extended scale, outside of the fancy of the writers and readers of certain books; the writers seem to have created her, and the readers believe in her.... The New Woman is the type of woman whom fictive art is just now dealing with, because she amuses, and because she is easier to do than the woman with less salient characteristics." By the end of the essay, Howells recanted somewhat, admitting that contemporary women "wish to know rather more of all sorts of things than they used," but he still insisted that her fictional counterpart had a distinguishable and conventional identity conferred on her by her self-dramatizing poses:

> She is distinguished, among those who have imagined her, from former phases of the eternal womanly. She is not what used to be called the woman of the period, she is by no means what used to be called fast, even in the less reproachful sense of the word. She is supposed to have certain views of marriage; she is supposed to have asked herself what her status would be if there was no marriage, in rare and ex-

treme cases she is supposed to have tried to find out. Whether she is for the enlargement of her civic rights or not, as a rule, it would not be easy to say; but she takes herself seriously, and she wishes to be thought serious when she does not take herself seriously.[13]

One vehicle for the exhibition of the New Woman's views was the dialogue novel, for the genre gave her the opportunity to express herself at length. We see her as a major character in Hunt's books and as a minor character in Anstey's *Lyre and Lancet* —a novel about the social complications that occur when a poet and a veterinarian are each assumed to be the other. Another form in which the New Woman could be exhibited was the novel that contrasted the New Woman and her traditional sister. The form doubtlessly owes much to such earlier pairings as the Good and Bad Heroines, the Light and Dark Ladies, the Spiritual and Sensuous Women, but in the nineties the contrast is distinguished by the fact that the author thinks of his (or more usually her) characters as exponents in the contemporary discussion of the role of women. The first novel to use this contrast was a somewhat earlier book: Olive Schreiner's *The Story of an African Farm,* published in 1883 and an international best seller by 1887.[14] Although there is no evidence that James read this novel, it inspired similar works of fiction, and he probably knew some of them. A somewhat cryptic reference to Sarah Grand (Frances Elizabeth MacFall) in one of James's "London" columns in *Harper's Weekly* suggests that he was familiar with her best seller of 1893, *The Heavenly Twins.*[15] And it would have been difficult for him to escape knowledge of the work of an old friend, Eliza Lynn Linton. As a journalist, Linton had addressed herself to feminist subjects from the sixties on. In the nineties, she dealt harshly with the New Woman, castigating her in periodical articles (where she appears as "the Wild Woman") and in several novels, of which *The New Woman: In Haste and at Leisure* is representative. By combining a sensational topical issue with a conservative moral viewpoint, Linton attracted a large following and merits our attention now as, according to one modern critic, "a sound and faithful register of the times in which she lived."[16]

These novels of contrasting women illuminate *The Awkward Age* by presenting character types against which James's young heroines, Aggie—the ward of one of Mrs. Brook's friends—and Nanda, can be profitably evaluated. In spite of the fact that Schreiner and Grand, unlike Linton, considered themselves feminists, all three depict the traditional woman as a passive, suffering individual and the New Woman as a bold but tormented person who must come to terms with marriage whether she wishes to or not—thus giving substance to Howells's generalization. Schreiner's Em is limited by an "idea of love [that] was only service"[17] and so accepts a loveless marriage; her New Woman, Lyndall, refuses marriage on principle but having done so finds no place for herself in society and symbolically dies after the birth of her child. Grand's heroines both marry men who had been rakes in their youths. Edith Beale, who does not understand her husband's past, innocently believes that if he has been a bad man she can reform him, discovers she cannot, and dies after having given birth to a syphilitic child. Evadne Frayling, on the other hand, is a self-educated feminist, though more domestically inclined than Lyndall. When she learns of her husband's past, she refuses conjugal relations with him and is finally freed by his death to marry a good man whom she loves. Linton's New Woman, Phoebe Barrington, joins a radical feminist club and refuses to live outside London with her husband, Sherrard. He falls in love with Edith Armytage, a "maiden born for love and duty and purity,"[18] and she too comes to love him. But both respect his marriage, both keep silent about their love, and both suffer. Phoebe eventually returns to Sherrard and learns to respect him and to accept her role as wife. It is worth remarking that none of these three authors depicts the New Woman as a career woman. Career women appear in the fiction of this period, but they are George Gissing's Odd Women who do not marry or Grant Allen's Woman Who Did who find work an economic necessity.[19] The New Woman who is relevant to *The Awkward Age* is the woman inspired by Schreiner's work, the woman with leisure and education and a sense that she is different from the women of the past.

James's young heroines significantly vary the patterns established by their predecessors. Aggie is a type sometimes found in English society of the period but in stunning contrast to her fictional sisters. Whereas Edith Beale's innocence results from a well-intended but foolishly principled upbringing, Aggie is the product of much calculation. Her guardian the Duchess explains that had the girl's parents lived, "She would have been brought up...under an anxious eye—that's the great point; privately, carefully, tenderly, and with what she was *not* to learn—till the proper time—looked after quite as much as the rest. I can only go on with her in that spirit..." (IX, 55). But laudable as the Duchess's fidelity to Aggie's parents and their traditions sounds, her interests are more practical. By raising her ward in the Continental manner as a *jeune fille,* the Duchess provides a public distraction from her own immorality. And even more important, in a society where a double standard exists, Aggie is the more attractive for her carefully cultivated innocence. In revealing metaphors, James has Longdon reflect that Aggie "had been deliberately prepared for consumption" by "being fed from the hand with the small sweet biscuit of unobjectionable knowledge" (IX, 238–39).

Given the "fast" society that Aggie lives in, her behavior after her marriage to Mitchy is not surprising—though it is both a funny and cynical comment on James's part. With the loss of innocence that her marriage brings comes also a loss of restraint and propriety. While the traditional woman passively accepts a loveless marriage, Aggie openly flirts with Lord Petherton, her guardian's lover and husband's friend. Mrs. Brook's set is both surprised and amused; the Duchess argues that this is what is to be expected when a sheltered girl marries; and only Nanda responds humanely: "Aggie's only trying to find out...what sort of a person she is. How can she ever have known? It was carefully, elaborately hidden from her..." (IX, 528). As Nanda's words bring home, Aggie has been cruelly used by those around her. Comparison with her fictional counterparts is instructive. Grand's and Linton's Ediths are simply counters that give their creators an opportunity to express the views they hold on the proper behavior of women: in one case, passive acceptance is pronounced wrong; in the other, proper. In contrast, James's Aggie, as Nanda helps us to see, is an implicit criticism of a society whose methods are manipulative, whose standards hypocritical. Although the Duchess speaks at length about how one should raise a girl, Aggie's plight speaks of more than what is proper female education and deportment. By treating a conventional type as expressive of specific social needs, James goes beyond the question of desirable female behavior and examines the corrupt values of the society he is depicting.

Nanda, too, is a contrast to her fictional counterparts. She is a New Woman in both her social awareness and her freedoms—to come and go as she likes, to visit whom she wishes, to conduct herself as she pleases. She does not have any kind of programatic sense of what woman's role should be as do Lyndall and Phoebe Barrington; instead, she is closer to Evadne Frayling and Moderna Maskelyne in simply understanding the social circle around her. But Lyndall, Phoebe, Evadne, and Moderna are what they are because

they have chosen to be so. Nanda, like Aggie, is a passive
victim of society and specifically of her mother.[20] Mrs.
Brook's virtual abandonment of her daughter by her refusal to accept her maternal role has left Nanda without
guidance or shelter. Tellingly, Nanda accounts for herself as
one who has been victimized, and her tone, as a result, is
always apologetic. She explains to Longdon, "One's just
what one *is*—is n't one? I don't mean so much...in one's
character or temper—for they have, have n't they? to be
what's called 'properly controlled'—as in one's mind and
what one sees and feels and the sort of thing one notices"
(IX, 230); to Van, "I can't help it any more than you can, can
I?" (IX, 344); and to Mitchy, "Does n't one become a sort of
a little drain-pipe with everything flowing through?" (IX,
358). It is no wonder that Van concludes that "Little Aggie's
really the sort of creature she [Nanda] would have liked to
be able to be" (IX, 310). Yet in a sense, Nanda is what Aggie
seems—a passive, accepting young woman, a traditional
Victorian lady—just as Aggie, finally, is what Nanda
seems—a modern young woman, heedless of all propriety.

Nanda's fate further bears out Van's observation. She is
rejected by the finicky Van himself, and in turn rejects the
nouveau riche Mitchy. She refuses his unvoiced proposal of
marriage by directing him to Aggie, and she declines his
hinted proposition that they become lovers in her last interview with him. Her values are indeed traditional, although
her circumstances have made her "The modern girl, the
product of our hard London facts and of her inevitable
consciousness of them just as they are..." (IX, 312). At the
very end of the novel, she is preparing to leave London
society and live with Mr. Longdon. Adoption, not marriage,
will be her lot. In this respect, too, she differs from her
fictional peers. At the ends of their stories, the other New
Women, with the exception of Lyndall, affirm the value of
marriage and thereby the social structure, and Lyndall's

death reflects Schreiner's inability to envision a career for her New Woman outside of marriage more forcefully than it suggests a rejection of society. But James is hardly posing a radical alternative to the plight of the New Woman, for Nanda is not to be counted with the defiant "rare and extreme cases" Howells mentioned. Midway through the novel, she senses what will become of her and tells Longdon, "I shall be one of the people who don't. I shall be at the end...one of those who have n't" (IX, 232). And she acquiesces to this fate as passively as she has accepted all else in her life. In her unsought, undesired celibacy, Nanda testifies to the power of her society.

Leon Edel has sentimentalized the end of *The Awkward Age,* seeing in it the culmination of James's self-therapy: "it seems in *The Awkward Age* that in removing Nanda from her mother's drawing room, Mr. Longdon can now do what Henry James had done all his life—harbor within his house, the house of the novelist's inner world, the spirit of a young adult female, worldly-wise and curious, possessing a treasure of unassailable virginity and innocence and able to yield to the masculine active world-searching side of James an ever-fresh and exquisite vision of feminine youth and innocence."[21] Without going so far as to see in Nanda evidence of her creator's androgyny, we can agree that the conclusion of *The Awkward Age* —almost by sleight of hand—serves James's private ends. While Nanda's retirement is a grim social commentary, it is also a fairy-tale ending. Mr. Longdon, described by Mrs. Brook as "the *oncle d'Amérique,* the eccentric benefactor, the fairy godmother" (IX, 181) is the deus ex machina who will take Nanda out of the circumstances that have shaped her. Her new life will be the antithesis of the life she has known. Its keynote will not be talk but silence. "Oh but when *have* we talked?" Longdon asks Nanda in their last interview; "When *have* n't we?" she responds (IX, 542–43). Having, in the words of one of the few contemporary critics who did justice to the novel, provided "a study of certain phases of London society to which other novelists of late years have borne awkward and incomplete testimony.... [so that] There now remains nothing to be told about the conversation and the complications in those circles where vast moral indifference is united to extreme intellectual acuteness,"[22] James thus grants Nanda the escape he earlier denied Maisie. It is appropriate to recall that he had given up London life for the relative solitude of Rye shortly before he wrote *The Awkward Age*.

Epilogue

The years encompassed by this study brought both failure and success to James. He clearly failed to win the popularity and concomitant financial reward that he once anticipated. As his fiction abundantly demonstrates, he understood which topical issues were of special interest to the general public and he knew the plot and character conventions with which popular writers clothed their discussions of those issues. But something happened when he turned his hand to such materials: "When he went abroad to gather garlic he came home with heliotrope" (XV, 211–12), as he had said of his artist in "The Next Time." The closest James ever came to the reasons for his difficulty was his belated recognition of the diversity of the reading public. In retrospect, we can see that with the careers of the great Victorian writers before him as models, James was looking for a more thoughtful hearing and congenial response than the mass reading audience of the late eighties and nineties could have given him. That audience, seeking, and finding in much popular writing, reassurance in an age of rapid social change, could hardly have found palatable James's persistent refusal to provide comfort. And as time went on and James's style grew increasingly idiosyncratic and complex, another barrier arose to discourage the average reader.

But something more was also at the root of James's difficulties. Contemporary reviewers frequently complained
that nothing happened in James's novels. Sometimes they
simply meant that nothing conventionally expected happened and lamented along with one of the straw men that
James sets up in "The Art of Fiction" the absence of "a
distribution at the last of prizes, pensions, husbands, wives,
babies, millions, appended paragraphs and cheerful remarks."[1] But often the reviewers understood some of what
prevented the conventional from happening: repeatedly
James is castigated for his habitual air of detachment, for
his refusal to be a partisan to his characters. One reviewer,
for example, summarizes his response to *The Princess
Casamassima:*

> Here is a novel which glances at some of the most important
> and far-reaching problems of the present, whose chief char-
> acters are conspirators plotting against the existing social
> order and discussing the wrongs of the oppressed,—mate-
> rial enough, one would think, for stirring incident, and am-
> ple opportunity for pointing a moral, expressing a con-
> viction, or delivering a warning. Yet the author's attitude is
> that of a mere observer: he preserves throughout the calm,
> superior air of one who has outgrown emotion and enthusi-
> asm; he looks upon his fellow-beings only as available liter-
> ary material. What does he believe? Does he hate? Does he
> love? If you prick him does he bleed? These questions can-
> not be answered from his work.[2]

Another writes similarly of *What Maisie Knew:*

> Its author exhibits not one ray of pity or dismay at this
> spectacle of a child with the pure current of its life thus
> poisoned at its source. To him she is merely the *raison d'être*
> of a curiously complicated situation, which he can twist and
> untwist for purposes of fiction. One feels in the reading that

every manly feeling, every possibility of generous sympathy, every comprehension of the higher standards, has become atrophied in Mr. James's nature from long disuse, and that all relation between him and his kind has perished except to serve him coldly by way of "material."[3]

Of course not all contemporary critics found James as disinterested as these two, and modern readers more often than not will argue for some degree of partisanship on James's part. Still, it is true that the overt sympathies and antipathies that characterize much popular fiction are absent from James's work, and the fiction of his London years is even more objective than usual. As all of the novels I have discussed illustrate, James's view of life was simply too dark to justify the moralistic and sentimental conclusions of popular fiction. He could not grant characters like Hyacinth Robinson and Maisie Farange happier fates without falsifying their experience—and his own vision—of contemporary life. In his unwillingness to do this, he was of course implicitly "expressing a conviction" about his times, but not one that the reviewer of *The Princess* whom I quote here—or the mass reading audience—could even recognize, let alone respond to.

While James's detachment must have counted in large part for his persistent failures with the public, that same quality accounts for the lasting, intrinsic success of those works shaped in response to the best-selling genres of the eighties and nineties. While a lesser writer with as profound a distaste for the social changes of the period and the greater dislocations that seemed to lie behind such changes would have been tempted to polemic or harangue, James never betrayed the artist in him. Using the literary language of his culture—its accepted plot and character conventions—he found a way to evaluate his society without giving excessive weight to the purely personal. In bringing together a variety of characters and plots in each work, he convincingly evoked the density and complexity of the world around him. By modifying received conventions and so playing off his plots and characters against his readers' expectations, he expressed his critical views within a framework that permitted him aesthetic distance. He had spoken once of his ambition "to leave a multitude of pictures of my time...a total having a certain value as observation and testimony." To do this, his stance would necessarily have to minimize the personal, as the words "observation" and "testimony" imply. In this ambition, James succeeded magnificently.

But it was not enough. James's move to Rye objectified an emotional disengagement with the best seller. He was tired of London life and its pressure and evidently equally tired of writing novels that were not only unremunerative but also emotionally constricting in their relative objectivity. The vigor with which the narrator of *The Sacred Fount* (1901)[4] is denounced suggests James's growing impatience with the role of detached observer—just as the indulgence with which Nanda Brookenham is treated at the end of *The Awkward Age* bespeaks a reawakened need for fiction in which he could invest himself as fully as he had years before in *The Portrait of a Lady*. We recall his response to Isabel Archer: "with her meagre knowledge, her inflated ideals, her confidence at once innocent and dogmatic, her temper at once exacting and indulgent, her mixture of curiosity and fastidiousness, of vivacity and indifference, her desire to look very well and to be if possible even better, her determination to see, to try, to know...she would be an easy victim of scientific criticism if she were not intended to awaken on the reader's part an impulse more tender and more purely expectant" (III, 69). Here James couples the detachment of the observer with the indulgence of a partisan. Isabel evokes and holds his sympathy because of her love for life and her vulnerability, because she is an outsider, and finally because she is a survivor. His years in London and their attendant difficulties could only have enhanced James's respect for these qualities.

When he returned to the international theme shortly after his move to Rye, he permitted himself an imaginative and emotional indulgence that he had not experienced for years. In *The Ambassadors* (1903), he relived the experience of the provincial coming in contact with a complex and sophisticated society; in *The Wings of the Dove* (1902), he once again reworked the story of the doomed but life-loving Minny Temple; and in *The Golden Bowl* (1904), he created his most tenacious survivor. In one sense, these novels all represent a real retreat on James's part, a turning away from the broad social issues that had occupied his attention for the last decade and a half. But the drama of the individual consciousness coming to terms not with the greater world but with its own strengths and limitations is so fully enacted in these novels that few modern readers regret the turning inward. Indeed, the magnitude of these late novels has diminished the achievement of the London fiction in the minds of most readers. For James, the change was energizing: the early years in Rye were the most productive of his life. The return to personally significant themes and the increased concentration on the individual consciousness, along with the gradual emergence of an audience sophisticated enough to appreciate what James was doing,[5] seems to have been what permitted him those final gestures of self-acceptance as a minority writer: the elaborate prefaces of the New York Edition and the volumes of the autobiography that present the author as an outsider from his childhood onward.

But I cannot conclude this study with this picture of James. As I suggested in the beginning, the Master was an assumed persona. It embodied some aspects of a complex author and concealed others. Although James rejoiced in the attention of the disciples whom he gathered around him toward the end of his life and delighted in speaking out as a revered authority on literary and cultural matters, his dream of an even wider fame never vanished. The insistence on dramatizing moral issues in melodramatic terms that look back to the great Victorian novelists in his late fiction, the pleasure he took in the popular adulation he received on his American tour, and the joy with which he seized the opportunity to put together a collected edition of his works on the plan of Balzac's *Comédie humaine* (and his deep disappointment at the commercial failure of the New York Edition) imply a refusal to believe that the limited role of the minority writer was all that was to be his in the end. The experience of the London years had taught him not to expect anything from the mass market of his time, but it had not foreclosed the future. Once in the midst of his troubles he had written to Howells, "Very likely...some day, all my buried prose will kick off its various tombstones at once."[6] It was his usual bravado, of course, but it was also a dream that redeemed that present and offered a compensation for a career that, with all its achievements, had failed of one particular success James had hoped for. In this matter, as in several others I have noted, bravado was ultimately not too far from prophecy.

NOTES

Chapter One

1. Virginia Harlow, *Thomas Sergeant Perry: A Biography and Letters to Perry from William, Henry, and Garth Wilkinson James* (Durham, N.C.: Duke University Press, 1950), p. 318. For letters similar in tone but more specific in reference see *Selected Letters of Henry James*, ed. Leon Edel (London: Rupert Hart-Davis, 1956), pp. 111–12; and *The Letters of Henry James*, vol. 1, ed. Percy Lubbock (New York: Scribner's, 1920), pp. 113–14 and 120–21.

2. "London," in *Essays in London and Elsewhere* (New York: Harper, 1893), pp. 20 and 8–9. In basic content, the 1888 and 1893 texts of this essay are the same, but the revisions in the later text reflect James's growing disenchantment with London and increase the pungency of his social criticism.

3. *Henry James: Letters*, vol. 2, ed. Leon Edel (Cambridge, Mass.: Harvard University Press, 1975), p. 335. This letter appears in Harlow, pp. 320–21, with the incorrect date of 1886.

4. *Letters of Henry James*, pp. 141–42.

5. Ibid., p. 166.

6. Ibid., p. 138.

7. Information on the growth of the reading public in this paragraph and the next is taken from Richard D. Altick, *The English Common Reader: A Social History of the Mass Reading Public 1800–1900* (1957; reprint, Chicago: University of Chicago Press, Phoenix Books, 1963), esp. pp. 294–317; Q. D. Leavis, *Fiction and the Reading Public* (1932; reprint, New York: Russell & Russell, 1965), esp. pp. 151–202; Jay Martin, *Harvests of Change: American Literature 1865–1914* (Englewood Cliffs, N.J.: Prentice-Hall, 1967), pp. 16–21; Adrian Poole, *Gissing in Context* (London: Macmillan, 1975), pp. 105–35; and Raymond Williams, *The Long Revolution* (1961; reprint, Harmondsworth, England: Penguin, 1975), pp. 177–94.

8. *The Popular Book: A History of America's Literary Taste* (1950; reprint, Berkeley: University of California Press, 1963), p. 185. Frank Luther Mott, *Golden Multitudes: The Story of Best Sellers in*

the United States (New York: Macmillan, 1947), pp. 204–06, also discusses the late-nineteenth-century interest in book sales.

9. Hart, *The Popular Book,* p. 184.

10. *The Novel: What It Is* (New York: Macmillan, 1893), pp. 20, 22–23, 86–87.

11. "The Art of Fiction: A Lecture Delivered at the Royal Institution, April 25, 1884," in *The Art of Fiction* by Walter Besant and Henry James (Boston: DeWolfe, Fiske, 1884), pp. 10, 29.

12. "The Art of Fiction," *Longman's,* September 1884, pp. 507, 510, 509, 518, 519, and 520.

13. Jacques Barzun ("Henry James, Melodramatist," *Kenyon Review* 5 [1943], reprinted in *The Question of Henry James: A Collection of Critical Essays,* ed. F. W. Dupee [New York: Henry Holt, 1945], pp. 254–66) and Peter Brooks (*The Melodramatic Imagination: Balzac, Henry James, Melodrama, and the Mode of Excess* [New Haven: Yale University Press, 1975], pp. 153–97) consider James's need to articulate moral conflict as the basis of his propensity to melodrama—a way of thinking and writing, both critics note, that he shares with earlier writers.

14. See John Goode, "The Art of Fiction: Walter Besant and Henry James," in *Tradition and Tolerance in Nineteenth-Century Fiction: Critical Essays on Some English and American Novels,* ed. David Howard, John Lucas, and John Goode (London: Routledge & Kegan Paul, 1966), pp. 243–81; and Mark Spilka, "Henry James and Walter Besant: 'The Art of Fiction' Controversy," *Novel* 6 (1972–73): 101–19. Both critics emphasize James's break with tradition in his essay.

15. The works alluded to in this paragraph are Leon Edel, *Henry James: The Middle Years, 1882–1895* (Philadelphia: Lippincott, 1962) and *Henry James: The Treacherous Years, 1895–1901* (Philadelphia: Lippincott, 1969); Maxwell Geismar, *Henry James and the Jacobites* (1962; reprint, New York: Hill & Wang, 1965); Edmund Wilson, "The Ambiguity of Henry James," *Hound and Horn* 7 (1933–34), reprinted with revisions and additions of 1938, 1948, and 1959 in *A Casebook on Henry James's "The Turn of the Screw,"* ed. Gerald Willen, 2d ed. (New York: Crowell, 1969), pp. 115–53; F. W. Dupee, *Henry James* (1951; reprint, Garden

City, N.J.: Doubleday, 1956); Oscar Cargill, *The Novels of Henry James* (1961; reprint, New York: Hafner, 1971); Sergio Perosa, *Henry James and the Experimental Novel* (Charlottesville: University Press of Virginia, 1978); Lyall H. Powers, *Henry James and the Naturalist Movement* (East Lansing: Michigan State University Press, 1971); Walter Isle, *Experiments in Form: Henry James's Novels, 1896–1901* (Cambridge, Mass.: Harvard University Press, 1968); Joseph Wiesenfarth, *Henry James and the Dramatic Analogy: A Study of the Major Novels of the Middle Period* (New York: Fordham University Press, 1963); and Donald David Stone, *Novelists in a Changing World: Meredith, James, and the Transformation of English Fiction in the 1880's* (Cambridge, Mass.: Harvard University Press, 1972).

16. See William T. Stafford's annual essays in *American Literary Scholarship* and Adeline R. Tinter, "Henry James Criticism: A Current Perspective," *American Literary Realism: 1870–1910* 7 (1974): 158–68.

17. "Du Maurier and London Society," *Century*, May 1883, p. 64. This essay was reprinted in *Partial Portraits*, 1888, under the title "George Du Maurier."

18. *Henry James—the Lessons of the Master: Popular Fiction and Personal Style in the Nineteenth Century* (Chicago: University of Chicago Press, 1975).

19. Alfred R. Ferguson, "The Triple Quest of Henry James: Fame, Art, and Fortune," *American Literature* 27 (1955–56): 475–98, convincingly attacks the all too prevalent myth that James was above an interest in making money.

20. Crawford, *The Novel*, p. 10.

21. *Selected Letters*, p. 109. See Harlow, p. 316, for similar remarks addressed to Perry. James did not get $500 per installment; he settled for something closer to $350 a month; see Edel, *The Middle Years*, p. 119.

22. *Letters of Henry James*, p. 135.

23. Ibid., p. 162; for similar comments see ibid., pp. 176, 206–07; and *The Notebooks of Henry James*, ed. F. O. Matthiessen and Kenneth B. Murdock (1947; reprint, New York: Oxford University Press, 1961), p. 99.

24. *Letters of Henry James*, p. 230.
25. Ibid., pp. 317–18.
26. Ibid., p. 170.

Chapter Two

1. *Henry James: Letters*, p. 365.
2. Edel, *The Middle Years*, pp. 19–78, discusses James's visits to America and his eagerness to return to London.
3. *Mediums, and Spirit-Rappers, and Roaring Radicals: Spiritualism in American Literature, 1850–1900* (Urbana: University of Illinois Press, 1972), pp. 190–222; my quotation is from p. 191. Also see Robert Emmet Long, *The Great Succession: Henry James and the Legacy of Hawthorne* (Pittsburgh: University of Pittsburgh Press, 1979), pp. 117–57, for a discussion of the way James transformed Hawthorne's themes into his own updated critique of American democracy.
4. James wrote to his brother William about *The Bostonians* shortly after the serialization had run its course: "The whole thing is too long and dawdling. This came from the fact (partly) that I had the sense of knowing terribly little about the kind of life I had attempted to describe—and felt a constant pressure to make the picture substantial by thinking it out—pencilling and 'shading.' I was afraid of the reproach (having *seen* so little of the whole business treated of,) of being superficial and cheap...." Quoted in F. O. Matthiessen, *The James Family Including Selections from the Writings of Henry James, Senior, William, Henry, and Alice James* (1947; reprint, New York: Knopf, 1961), p. 329.
5. Andrew Sinclair, *The Emancipation of the American Woman* (1965; reprint, New York: Harper & Row, Colophon, 1966), p. 264, suggests similarities between Victoria Woodhull and Verena; Sara deSaussure Davis, "Feminist Sources in *The Bostonians*," *American Literature* 50 (1978–79): 570–87, argues that "Susan Anthony, Whitelaw Reid, and Anna Dickinson are transmogrified into Olive Chancellor, Basil Ransom, and Verena Tarrant" (p. 580); and Kerr, *Mediums*, pp. 196–203, finds similarities between Verena and the trance-speaking Cora L. V. Hatch. Sin-

clair, pp. 117–96, and Eleanor Flexner, *Century of Struggle: The Woman's Rights Movement in the United States* (1959; reprint, New York: Atheneum, 1973), pp. 142–55, provide good discussions of the woman's movement in the 1870s.

6. Peter Buitenhuis, *The Grasping Imagination: The American Writings of Henry James* (Toronto: University of Toronto Press, 1970), pp. 142–45, 158, discusses James's use of Daudet in *The Bostonians*. Other critics suggest additional sources: Cargill, *The Novels of Henry James*, pp. 125–29, notes the influences of Howells (*Dr. Breen's Practice*), Hawthorne (*The Blithedale Romance*), *Antigone*, and *L'Évangéliste;* Powers, *Henry James and the Naturalist Movement*, pp. 53–58, covers the same ground with special emphasis on Daudet and adds Howells's *The Undiscovered Country* to the list; Stone, *Novelists in a Changing World*, pp. 259–82, discusses elements of Victorian fiction in the novel; and see Kerr, *Mediums*, pp. 190–222, and Long, *The Great Succession*, pp. 117–57. As I will argue, the major configurations of *The Bostonians* seem to be those of popular fiction.

7. *Henry James: Letters*, pp. 359–60.

8. In his notebook, James described the relationship between Verena and Olive as "a study of one of those friendships between women which are so common in New England" (*N*, p. 47). It is not clear from this that he originally intended the relationship to be the unhealthy one it is in the novel. I have been unable to find out when the present-day term "New England marriage," a euphemism for a lesbian relationship, first came into use. Most critics approve Verena's marriage; two who do not are Judith Fetterley, *The Resisting Reader: A Feminist Approach to American Fiction* (Bloomington: Indiana University Press, 1978), pp. 101–53, who, while fully aware of both Ransom's and Olive's limitations, notes that Olive genuinely loves Verena, whereas Ransom does not; and David Howard, "The Bostonians," in *The Air of Reality: New Essays on Henry James*, ed. John Goode (London: Methuen, 1972), pp. 72–79, who argues that Verena's marriage represents a loss of vitality for herself and for the American scene of which she is a part.

9. Irving Howe, Introduction to *The Bostonians*, by Henry James (New York: Random House, Modern Library, 1956), pp.

v–xxviii, discusses the feminist movement in *The Bostonians* as an aspect of post–Civil War American life. In characterizing that life as James dramatizes it, he focuses, not on conflict as I do, but on the depersonalization of life: "In the mass industrial society that was coming into existence toward the end of the nineteenth century, the role of the sexes with regard to one another was no longer clear, the centers of authority and affection had become blurred, the continuity of family culture was threatened, but most important of all: the idea of what it meant to be human had come into question. All that we have since associated with industrial society was moving into sight—call it depersonalization or *anomie*, the sapping of individuality or the loss of tradition" (p. xviii).

10. Robert A. Lively, *Fiction Fights the Civil War: An Unfinished Chapter in the Literary History of the American People* (Chapel Hill: University of North Carolina Press, 1957), notes: "The [Civil War] theme's greatest popularity began during the middle eighties..." (p. 21). The *Atlantic* observed the same thing and offered an explanation: "It is pretty clear that we are entering upon a period in our literature when the war for the Union is to play a highly interesting part. Until lately we have lacked the requisite historical perspective" ("Recent American Fiction," January 1885, p. 123).

11. "*The Bostonians:* Creation and Revision," *Bulletin of the New York Public Library* 73 (1969): 300–01.

12. This reconciliatory mood is evident in the "Studies in the South" series which ran intermittently in the *Atlantic* in 1882 and 1883; similarly the *Century* introduced its "Battles and Leaders of the Civil War" series in 1884 by noting one of its central purposes as being "to soften controversy with that better understanding of each other, which comes to comrades in arms when personal feeling has dissipated, and time has proven how difficult are the duties and how changeable are the events of war—how enveloped in accident and mystery" ("Topics of the Time: Battles and Leaders of the Civil War," October 1884, p. 943).

13. *Heiress of all the Ages: Sex and Sentiment in the Genteel Tradition* (Minneapolis: University of Minnesota Press, 1959), p. 31.

14. Harlow, *Thomas Sergeant Perry*, p. 309.

15. *An Original Belle* (1885; reprint, New York: Collier, 1902), p. 518.

16. Wasserstrom, *Heiress*, pp. 31–34, suggests that James was drawing on types established by the Civil War fiction of the 1860s. He misses the point that James was insisting on regional differences at a time when the tendency of popular fiction was to blur those differences. Larzer Ziff, *The American 1890's: Life and Times of a Lost Generation* (1966; reprint, New York: Viking, 1968), pp. 51–52, speaks of the conclusion of James's novel as a consciously ironic reversal of the conventional conversion to the Northern point of view. This reading, like Wasserstrom's, does not relate *The Bostonians* to the fiction of the 1880s. James's impact lies not only in his having a Southerner triumph but also in insisting on Verena's conversion to Ransom's point of view in a period in which reconciliation, not conversion, is standard. James may, of course, have recalled the early Civil War novel when he wrote *The Bostonians*, but the social and literary context of his novel remind us that his reversion to those early patterns must be understood in terms of his reaction to America in the eighties. It should also be noted that James's ideas of regional types came from life as well as literature. Edel, *The Middle Years*, pp. 140, 143, notes that Lucius Q. C. Lamar and Elizabeth Peabody contributed to the characterizations of Ransom and Miss Birdseye, for example.

17. Mississippi is not Virginia, a fact which James did not forget but which critics sometimes do. Powers claims that "one is made to feel that behind him [Ransom] lies a long pedigree, a gentle society, traditions and conventions and a way of life not vastly different from the life of Europe as the Jamesian heroine finds it" (p. 84). Philip Rahv (Introduction to *The Bostonians*, by Henry James [New York: Dial Press, 1945], p. ix) and Lionel Trilling (Introduction to *The Bostonians*, by Henry James [London: Lehmann, 1952], p. xii) also offer notable overestimations of Ransom's character. Ransom might better be compared with some of Mark Twain's Mississippi Valley aristocrats.

18. *The Bostonians* (New York: Random House, Modern Library, 1956), pp. 4–5. Subsequent references are to this edition and are incorporated in my text.

19. Edel, *The Middle Years,* p. 145.
20. Matthiessen, *The James Family,* p. 327.
21. *Literary World,* 17 April 1886, p. 137. Because of Osgood's bankruptcy, Macmillan published *The Bostonians,* so the first American edition was actually printed in England. The note in the *Literary World* alluded to this fact in further remarking on the popular indifference to James's novel: "It was said that the American edition of this book was to have been shipped from London on the ill-fated 'Oregon,' but that, by what was deemed a happy accident, the supply was delayed a day or two. Had this not happened the insurance companies might perhaps have proved better purchasers than the general public." See the reviews in the *Nation,* 13 May 1886, pp. 407–08, and the *Atlantic* ("James, Crawford, and Howells," [by H. E. Scudder]), June 1886, pp. 851–53, which are thoughtful and critical but not gratuitously cruel.

Chapter Three

1. *My Apprenticeship* (1926; reprint, Harmondsworth, England: Penguin, 1971), p. 186.
2. Harlow, *Thomas Sergeant Perry,* p. 319.
3. *The Novels of Henry James,* p. 149.
4. Edel, *The Middle Years,* p. 138, notes that James intended to write a six-part serial and wrote a thirteen-part serial instead. *The Bostonians* was serialized in the *Century* from February 1885 to February 1886; *The Princess Casamassima* overlapped it, appearing in the *Atlantic* from September 1885 to October 1886.
5. Cargill, *The Novels of Henry James,* p. 149. James reviewed *Virgin Soil* for the *Nation,* 26 April 1877. Critics frequently speak of the Dickensian quality of *The Princess* too, but as I will suggest, there are more immediate influences.
6. Matthiessen, *The James Family,* p. 327.
7. P. J. Keating, *The Working Classes in Victorian Fiction* (London: Routledge & Kegan Paul, 1971), offers a useful discussion of the working-class novel. He considers both the plot conventions I discuss as examples of the "working-class romance,"

and he notes the preponderance of this type in the eighties. See esp. pp. 43–52.

8. *Fame and Fiction: An Enquiry into Certain Popularities* (London: Grant Richards, 1901), p. 145. Bennett was among the first to analyze the mass market. His aim in this book was "to explain to the minority why the majority likes or dislikes certain modern novelists" (p. 6).

9. *"The Princess Casamassima,"* in *The Liberal Imagination: Essays on Literature and Society* (1950; reprint, New York: Doubleday, Anchor Books, 1953), pp. 58–61.

10. Howells's review in *Harper's* ("Editor's Study," April 1887, p. 829) and the review in *Lippincott's* (February 1887, p. 359) compare *The Princess* to W. H. Mallock's *The Old Order Changes* (1886); Julia Wedgwood reviewed Mallock's book, Besant's *Children of Gibeon,* and *The Princess* together in the *Contemporary Review* (December 1886, pp. 899–901) but drew a comparison only between *The Princess* and the briefly mentioned *Landon Deecroft: A Socialistic Novel* (1886), by Laon Ramsey (Ramsden Balmforth).

11. W. H. Tilley, *The Background of "The Princess Casamassima"* (Gainesville: University of Florida Press, 1961), discusses *Virgin Soil,* James's travels in a France which still bore evidence of the Revolution and the Commune of 1871, as well as James's probable readings in the *London Times* as sources for *The Princess.*

12. Irving Howe, "The Political Vocation," in *Politics and the Novel* (1957), reprinted in *Henry James: A Collection of Critical Essays,* ed. Leon Edel (Englewood Cliffs, N.J.: Prentice-Hall, 1963), pp. 161–67; Tilley, *Background of "The Princess,"* p. 24; Trilling, *"The Princess Casamassima,"* pp. 64–71.

13. This is not to say that James literally believed that revolution was imminent but rather that he sensed a profoundly disturbing reality beneath the surface of life. See Brooks, *The Melodramatic Imagination,* esp. pp. 168–79, and Graham Greene, "Henry James: The Private Universe," in *The English Novelists,* ed. Derek Verschoyle (1936), and "Henry James: The Religious Aspect," in *Contemporary Essays, 1933,* ed. Sylva Norman (1933), both reprinted in *The Lost Childhood and Other Essays,* New York: Viking, 1952, pp. 21–30 and 31–39, for discussions of James's sense of evil as something beyond what is directly knowable.

14. The name "Muniment" first appears in *The Princess* at the end of chap. 7, a section that appeared in the October 1885 issue of the *Atlantic*. Is it possible that Besant condescended to borrow from James?

15. George Monteiro, *Henry James and John Hay: The Record of a Friendship* (1963; reprint, Providence: Brown University Press, 1965), p. 155, quotes this letter at length; it also appears in *Letters of Henry James*, p. 104, with Crawford's name deleted. James asks Howells not to mention his feelings to anyone "as it will be set down to green-eyed jealousy," a request that suggests that James in fact was jealous. He had reason to be: Monteiro notes that in the two weeks after publication, *To Leeward* sold more than 7,000 copies; it was to take *The Portrait of a Lady* eleven years to match this (p. 155).

16. *Letters of Henry James*, p. 124 (December 1886).

17. Edel, *The Middle Years*, pp. 190–92, and Trilling, "*The Princess Casamassima*," pp. 73–76. Both critics point out similarities between Hyacinth and James and between the surrogate family James provides for Hyacinth and his own family. But the surrogate family, as I note, is a standard feature of the working-class novel, and while James may have been drawn to the convention because it fit his personal needs, the choice must also be recognized as a conscious artistic choice.

18. Powers, *Henry James and the Naturalist Movement*, pp. 88–123, offers the most extensive discussion of *The Princess* as a naturalistic novel but does little beyond noting its obvious stress on environment and heredity.

19. *Workers in the Dawn*, 2 vols. (1880; reprint, New York: Doubleday Doran, 1935), 2: 158.

20. Trilling, "*The Princess Casamassima*," pp. 81–82.

21. The first edition text reads: "It rose before him like a kind of backward accusation of his mother; to suffer it to start out in the life of her son was in a manner to place her own forgotten, redeemed pollution again in the eye of the world" ([London: Macmillan, 1886], III, 231). This version, which does not emphasize the deformity of the mother, seems more appropriate to Hyacinth's protective mood at this point in the novel; in this

frame of mind, he would be apt to deemphasize his mother's failings.

22. For attempts to come to terms with this difficulty, see John P. O'Neill, *Workable Design: Action and Situation in the Fiction of Henry James* (Port Washington, N.Y.: Kennikat Press, 1973), pp. 49–69, who argues that "What James attempts in the two books which remain [after Hyacinth's return from the Continent] is to make of Hyacinth the emblem of the Jamesian consciousness, and to try to demonstrate the superiority of this power when judged against the pretensions of a collective morality and political action" (p. 66) represented by the Princess and Muniment, but notes that this is not a successful strategy on James's part because as James handles it, it reduces Hyacinth to a passive victim and undercuts our respect for him (p. 68); and see J. A. Ward, *The Search for Form: Studies in the Structure of James's Fiction* (Chapel Hill: University of North Carolina Press, 1967), pp. 114–40, who argues that "One of James's intentions is to equate revolution and betrayal" but also notes that "the public theme and the private theme do not quite coalesce" (p. 123) and that the concluding section of the book reduces rather than extends James's social (public) theme.

23. John Goode, "The Art of Fiction: Walter Besant and Henry James," pp. 278–81, states the point slightly differently by noting the lack of historical cogency in James's novel and in other working-class novels of the period: in their opposition of laborers and aristocrats instead of labor and capital they are evading social reality for a more comfortable and familiar fiction.

24. Monteiro, *Henry James and John Hay*, p. 40. In a similar letter to Perry (also 1884), James looks disparagingly at best sellers in America, including *To Leeward*, and notes that one of them is "the Breadwinners (the cleverness of which I don't contest)," a rather backhanded compliment under the circumstances (Harlow, *Thomas Sergeant Perry*, p. 316; Monteiro, *Henry James and John Hay*, p. 39).

Chapter Four

1. *Letters of Henry James*, p. 138.

2. Ibid. Roger Gard, ed., *Henry James: The Critical Heritage* (London: Routledge & Kegan Paul, 1968), notes, "the book reached a new low point in sales for a novel" (p. 553). He records two English printings of 500 and 2,000 and one American of 1,000.

3. Powers, *Henry James and the Naturalist Movement,* pp. 131, 155–58; Stone, *Novelists in a Changing World,* pp. 308–30; Edel, *The Middle Years,* pp. 261–62.

4. See the reviews in the *Athenaeum,* 26 July 1890, p. 124; *Murray's* ("Mr. Henry James"), November 1891, pp. 648, 650; and *Public Opinion* 13 September 1890, pp. 539–40.

5. *Nation,* 19 December 1878, p. 388.

6. *Macleod of Dare* (London: Macmillan, 1878), 1: 213.

7. James's letter to Mrs. Ward is quoted extensively in D. J. Gordon and John Stokes, "The Reference of *The Tragic Muse,*" in *The Air of Reality: New Essays on Henry James,* ed. John Goode (London: Methuen, 1972), p. 120.

8. See ibid., pp. 121–22, on the surprising popularity of Mrs. Ward's book; ibid., pp. 122–25, on Mary Anderson.

9. Edward Stone, *The Battle and the Books: Some Aspects of Henry James* (Athens: Ohio University Press, 1964), pp. 93–112, discusses a number of similarities between James's book and Black's. Critics who discuss *Miss Bretherton* are Cargill, *The Novels of Henry James,* pp. 184–86; Powers, *Henry James and the Naturalist Movement,* pp. 131–32; and Gordon and Stokes, "The Reference of *The Tragic Muse,*" pp. 119–22. Edel, *The Middle Years,* pp. 254, 260, discusses possible life models for James's characters; Edel's suggestion that James drew on actual people for his characters does not, of course, invalidate the claim that his characters were first suggested by other works of fiction.

10. "The Reference of *The Tragic Muse,*" p. 118.

11. *Miss Bretherton* (London: Macmillan, 1884), p. 187.

12. *The Tragic Muse* was serialized in the *Atlantic* from January 1889 to May 1890; "An Animated Conversation" appeared in *Scribner's* in March 1889. My quotation is from p. 372.

13. In his New York Edition preface James speaks of Miriam's counterproposal as sincere and of Peter's response as indicative of his limitations (VII, xix–xx). This is another instance in which

the preface does not accord with the novel. See my discussion at the beginning of Chapter Four and note 14 below.

14. The evolution James describes in his preface begins with the Nick-Julia story: "I...must in fact practically have always had, the happy thought of some dramatic picture of the 'artist-life' and of the difficult terms on which it is at the best secured and enjoyed, the general question of its having to be not altogether easily paid for....The young man who should 'chuck' admired politics, and of course some other admired object with them, would be all very well; but he would n't be enough—therefore what should one say to some other young man who would chuck something and somebody else, admired in their way too?" (VII, v, vii–viii). Edel, *The Middle Years*, p. 254, suggests that the "case" of Cyril Flowers, a man with artistic interests, a politically ambitious wife, and consequently a political career, may have provided the inspiration for James's complementary plot. He entertains no doubts that the story of the actress came first.

15. Cargill, *The Novels of Henry James*, pp. 191–93, 200–01, summarizes some of the debate over Nash's origin. Candidates for the original include Henry James, Sr., James himself, Herbert Pratt, and Cargill's own favorite, Oscar Wilde. Cargill is the only critic who considers a possible literary antecedent for Nash, but he does no more than suggest that the fading of Nash's portrait might be an allusion to Wilde's *The Picture of Dorian Gray* (p. 193). This, however, is an impossibility, since *Dorian Gray* was first published in July 1890 in *Lippincott's*, whereas the serialization of *The Tragic Muse* ended in May of the same year.

16. *The Martyrdom of Madeline* (London: Chatto & Windus, 1882), 2: 175. Jerome Hamilton Buckley, *The Victorian Temper: A Study in Literary Culture* (1951; reprint, New York: Random House, Vintage Books, 1964), pp. 161–64 and 182–83, discusses Buchanan's reactions to aestheticism. He also provides a useful discussion of aestheticism in the eighties, pp. 207–25.

Buchanan further claims our attention. In an essay, "The Modern Young Man as Critic," he noted the extent of James's immersion in popular culture: "He is secretly indifferent about all the gods, dead and living. He takes us into his confidence, welcomes us into his study; and we find that the faces on the walls are those, not of a pantheon, but of the comic newspaper and the circulating library. He appears to recognise the modern Sybil in George Eliot; and why indeed should he not take that triumphant Talent seriously, when the inspiration of his childhood was the picture gallery in *Punch,* when he sees a profound social satirist in Mr. du Maurier, and when he can fall prone before the masterpieces of that hard-bound genius *in posse,* Mr. Robert Louis Stevenson? These, then, are the glorious discoveries of the young man's omniscience—George Eliot, Alphonse Daudet, Flaubert, du Maurier, Mr. Punch, and the author of 'Treasure Island.' With these, one is bound to say, he is, like all well-bred Americans, thoroughly at home" (*Universal Review,* March 1889, p. 356). I take exception to Buchanan's tone but not his point. See note 20 below.

17. *Miss Brown* (1884; reprint, New York: George Munroe, Seaside Library, n.d.), p. 111. See Vineta Colby, *The Singular Anomaly: Women Novelists of the Nineteenth Century* (1970; reprint, New York: New York University Press, 1972), pp. 253–60, for an account of James's initial dismay and ultimate tact in responding to the book. He found the conclusion of the book false—Anne Brown marries her aesthetic mentor, whom she has come to hate, in order to save him from himself—and found the handling of the aesthetic circle offensive, especially in its emphasis on sex.

18. *The North Wall* (Glasgow: Wilson & McCormick, 1885), p. 18.

19. Amy Cruse, *The Victorians and Their Reading* (1935; reprint, Boston: Houghton Mifflin, 1936), pp. 384–88, discusses some of the popular manifestations of aestheticism.

20. "Du Maurier and London Society," *Century,* May 1883, p. 63. *The Tragic Muse* also includes a tribute to the *Punch* cartoons; see VIII, 212. In one of Du Maurier's cartoons ("Maudle on the Choice of a Profession"), Maudle tells a "Philistine from the country" who is concerned with what her son should be, "Why should he *Be* anything? Why not let him remain for ever content to *Exist Beautifully?*" (*Punch,* 12 February 1881, p. 62). Shades of Gabriel Nash. I suspect that a number of the social complications in James's novels were inspired, at least in part, by *Punch* cartoons. In another ("Where the Shoe Pinches"), for example, the follow-

ing exchange takes place: "*Eldest Daughter*. 'I think you might let me come out, Mamma! I'm Twenty, you know, and surely I've finished my Education!' *Festive Mamma (by no means prepared to act the part of Chaperone and Wallflower)*. 'Not yet, my Love. Society is so hollow! I really must preserve that sweet Girlish Freshness of yours a little while longer!'" (*Punch*, 4 December 1880, p. 258). We see the same situation, wonderfully transfigured, in *The Awkward Age*.

21. James also knew the poseur who was closer to decadence than aestheticism and perhaps drew on his own revulsion in describing the suspicion Nash encounters. In 1884 he read Huysmans's *A Rebours*, which he found to possess "all the signs of complete decadence—elaborate & incurable rot" (Harlow, *Thomas Sergeant Perry*, p. 317, to Perry). He may also have seen George Moore's *Confessions of a Young Man* (1886), which includes an attack on James for his prudery. James had apparently met Moore and corresponded with him on the subject of fiction before *Confessions* was written; under these circumstances, it is quite probable that he knew of Moore's book and his subsequent nastiness. Susan Dick supplies this information about the relation between the two men in the notes to her edition of *Confessions* (Montreal: McGill-Queen's University Press, 1972), pp. 251–52, nn. 5 and 10; she cites Moore's *Avowals* (1904) as her source. Edel's biography does not mention that James was acquainted with Moore in the eighties.

22. Two critics whose approaches emphasize the thematic unity of *The Tragic Muse* are Kenneth Graham, *Henry James: The Drama of Fulfillment* (London: Oxford University Press, Clarendon Press, 1975), pp. 79–126, who examines the various kinds of talent in the novel; and Dorothea Krook, *The Ordeal of Consciousness in Henry James* (1962; reprint, Cambridge: Cambridge University Press, 1967), pp. 62–105, who looks particularly at James's examination of the English character.

Chapter Five

1. "Henry James: The Dramatic Years," in *Guy Domville*, by Henry James, ed. Leon Edel (1949; reprint, Philadelphia: Lip-

pincott, Keystone Books, 1960), pp. 48–65. Another, similar version of this essay precedes *The Complete Plays of Henry James*, ed. Leon Edel (Philadelphia: Lippincott, 1949), pp. 19–69. Edel's discussions of James's playwriting in *The Middle Years*, pp. 39–41, 279–99, and in *The Treacherous Years*, pp. 19–88, place less emphasis on the compensatory nature of James's activity.

2. For useful discussions of the well-made play see Francis Fergusson, *The Idea of a Theater, a Study of Ten Plays*; *The Art of Drama in a Changing Perspective* (1949; reprint, Garden City, N.J.: Doubleday, Anchor Books, n.d. [1954]), pp. 77–80 and 246–47, and John Russell Taylor, *The Rise and Fall of the Well-Made Play* (London: Methuen, 1967), pp. 11–91.

3. "After the Play," *New Review*, June 1889, p. 41.

4. *The Eighteen Nineties: A Review of Art and Ideas at the Close of the Nineteenth Century* (1913; reprint, New York: Capricorn, 1966), p. 212.

5. Crawford, *The Novel*, p. 22.

6. *The Pen and the Book* (London: Thomas Burleigh, 1899), pp. 107–98.

7. "On the Occasion of *Hedda Gabler*," *New Review*, June 1891, p. 526.

8. *Complete Plays*, pp. 349, 347. In the preface to the first volume of *Theatricals* (1894; *Tenants* [1890] and *Disengaged* [1892]), James similarly remarks that these plays "doubtless missed their way through an anxious excess of simplicity" (*Complete Plays*, p. 255).

9. *Selected Letters*, pp. 125–26. *The Other House* was serialized in the *Illustrated London News*, 4 July to 26 September, 1896.

10. *Saturday Review*, 31 October 1896, p. 474. Also see the review in *Critic*, 28 November 1896, p. 335, for an enthusiastic response to the book because of its power and directness.

11. *The Country of the Blind and Other Stories* (London: Thomas Nelson, n.d. [1911]), pp. iv–vi.

12. James's letter is printed in part in *Letters of Henry James*, pp. 230–32 (my quotation is from p. 231), and in part in Edel, *The Treacherous Years*, pp. 94–95 (the list of magazines and publishers is on p. 95). James had complained as early as 1888 that publishers did not want his work (*Letters of Henry James*, p. 135), and

in the New York Edition preface to *The Tragic Muse* he complained, as I noted, that the novel had brought to an end for him
"the pleasant old custom of the 'running' of the novel" (VII, vi).

13. What exclusion from these magazines meant to James is
vividly suggested by his remarks in one of his "American Letter"
columns: "The intelligence and liberality with which a great
number of these [American magazines] are conducted, and the
remarkable extent of their diffusion, make them so representative of the conditions in which they circulate that they strike me
as speaking for their native public—comparing other publics and
other circulations—with a responsibility quite their own. There
are more monthly and quarterly periodicals in England—I for-
bear to go into the numerical relation, but they are certainly read
by fewer persons and take fewer pains to be read at all; and there
is in France a fortnightly publication—venerable, magnificent,
comprehensive—the mere view of the rich resources and honor-
able life of which endears it, throughout the world, to the mind
of the man of letters. But there is distinctly something more
usual and mutual in the established American patronage of
'Harper,' 'Scribner,' the 'Century,' the 'Cosmopolitan,' than in any
English patronage of anything of the monthly order or even than
in any patronage anywhere of the august *Revue des Deux Mondes*"
(*Literature*, 11 June 1898, p. 676).

14. See Thomas Beer, *The Mauve Decade: American Life at the
End of the Nineteenth Century* (1926; reprint, New York: Random
House, Vintage Books, 1961), pp. 150–73; John Tomsich, *A Genteel Endeavor: American Culture and Politics in the Gilded Age* (Stanford: Stanford University Press, 1971); and Ziff, *The American
1890's*, pp. 120–45, for discussions of American magazines in the
nineties; and Jackson, *The Eighteen Nineties*, pp. 45–51, for a
discussion of British magazines in the period.

15. One indication of the popularity of ghost stories in the
period is Jerome K. Jerome's burlesque, *Told after Supper*. Jerome
was well known as the author of the best-selling *Three Men in a
Boat* (1889) as well as other humorous sketches. In *Told after
Supper*, he observes "There is a good deal of similarity about our
ghostly experiences; but this of course is not our fault but the
fault of the ghosts, who never will try any new performances..."

(London: Leadenhall Press, 1891, pp. 16–17). He goes on to outline the several stories most common to the genre. For another contemporary response, see "Editor's Easy Chair," *Harper's*, September 1890, pp. 635–37, which comments on man's longstanding interest in ghost stories and notes both the perennial recurrence of many of the story types Jerome discusses and the extensive contemporary investigations of psychic phenomena.

16. For accounts of the way in which the short story took over the field formerly held by the massive Gothic novel, see Howard Phillips Lovecraft, *Supernatural Horror in Literature* (1927; reprint, New York: Dover, 1973); Peter Penzoldt, *The Supernatural in Fiction* (1952; reprint, New York: Humanities Press, 1965), pp. 67–164; and Dorothy Scarborough, *The Supernatural in Modern English Fiction* (New York: Putnam's, 1917), pp. 6–223.

17. See Martha Banta, *Henry James and the Occult: The Great Extension* (Bloomington: Indiana University Press, 1972), pp. 9–50; E. A. Sheppard, *Henry James and "The Turn of the Screw"* (Auckland: Auckland University Press, 1974), pp. 116–211; and Francis X. Roellinger, "Psychical Research and 'The Turn of the Screw,'" *American Literature* 20 (1948–49), reprinted in *The Turn of the Screw: An Authoritative Text, Backgrounds and Sources, Essays in Criticism,* ed. Robert Kimbrough (New York: Norton, 1966), pp. 132–42, for discussions of James's familiarity with the work of the Society for Psychical Research. Banta takes James at his word when he says that the work of the society did not inspire good fiction; both Sheppard and Roellinger argue that James nevertheless found much in the society's investigations that was usable.

18. Many of these stories are collected in *The Water Ghost and Others* (1894) and *Ghosts I Have Met and Some Others* (1898).

19. Introduction, *Soldiers Three*, by Rudyard Kipling (Leipzig: Heinemann & Balestier, 1891), pp. xix, xvii. James's introduction was first published early in 1891 as the introduction to *Mine Own People*, another collection of Kipling's stories.

20. "The Red Room," *Chap-Book*, 15 February 1896, p. 324.

21. *Letters of Henry James*, pp. 227–29; and see ibid., pp. 233–34 for similar remarks in another letter to William.

22. *Aspects and Impressions* (London: Cassell, 1922), pp. 34–35.

23. *The Treacherous Years*, p. 85.

24. "The Ambiguity of Henry James," pp. 133, 134.

25. *Henry James and the Jacobites*, pp. 129–83.

26. *The Treacherous Years*, p. 109; this is the thesis of the entire volume.

27. Ibid., pp. 260–67.

28. *Versions of Melodrama: A Study of the Fiction and Drama of Henry James, 1865–1897* (Berkeley: University of California Press, 1957), p. 69. Also see Perosa, *Henry James and the Experimental Novel*, pp. 3–76, for a discussion of James's shift from the pictorial, naturalistic method of the eighties to the scenic method of the nineties. Perosa's observation that James's change in method brought about a greater concentration on moral and psychological issues complements Levy's work.

29. *Letters of Henry James*, pp. 234.

30. Edel, *The Middle Years*, pp. 313–14, suggests that James's relationship with the young acolytes who began to surround him in the nineties is indirectly shown in the tales of literary life. In *The Treacherous Years*, p. 48, he is more specific, suggesting that "The Middle Years" "seems to reflect" James's intense relationship with Wolcott Balestier.

31. Not only do James's recent difficulties in the marketplace enter into "The Next Time," but an earlier failure with the public does as well. In his notebook entries on the story, James recalls that in 1876 he wrote a series of letters from Paris for the New York *Tribune* only to have his editor tell him they were not vulgar and "personal" enough. James claimed he could not produce anything worse than he had and so lost the job (*N*, pp. 180, 200–01). This experience is given to the artist in "The Next Time" too.

32. "Enoch Soames," in *Seven Men* (London: William Heinemann, 1919), p. 6.

33. *Miss Brown*, p. 17.

34. For James's acquaintance with Lee's and Gissing's work, see Chapters Four and Three. James sent a copy of *The Light that Failed* to Stevenson in Samoa observing, "I find it the most youthfully infirm of his [Kipling's] productions (in spite of great 'life',) much wanting in composition and in narrative and explicative, or even implicative, art" (*Henry James and Robert Louis Steven-*

son: A Record of Friendship and Criticism, ed. Janet Adam Smith [London: Rupert Hart-Davis, 1948], p. 202, letter of January 1891). In Kipling's defense it should be mentioned that the version of *The Light that Failed* that James read, that published in *Lippincott's* in January 1891, is weaker and more sentimental than the revised book version.

35. "The Pot Boiler," *Longman's*, October 1892, pp. 600–01.

Chapter Six

1. *What Maisie Knew* was serialized in the *Chap-Book*, 15 January to 1 August, 1897, and in a somewhat abridged form in the *New Review*, February to September, 1897.

2. Amy Cruse (*After the Victorians* [London: George Allen & Unwin, 1938], p. 49) and Samuel Hynes (*The Edwardian Turn of Mind* [Princeton: Princeton University Press, 1968], pp. 172–85) discuss the popularity of Marriage Question plays.

3. James refers to *The Masqueraders* in a letter of January 1895; see *Letters of Henry James*, p. 228. Edel, *The Treacherous Years*, mentions James's having seen *Lady Windermere's Fan* (p. 44), *A Woman of No Importance* (p. 46), and *The Second Mrs. Tanqueray* (p. 24).

4. Geismar, *Henry James and the Jacobites*, p. 147, claims that *Maisie* was first conceived of as a play, but I can find no evidence of this. But Geismar also notes, rightly I believe, the farcelike quality of James's novel (p. 152).

5. "The Ambiguity of Henry James," pp. 149–50.

6. *The Treacherous Years*, pp. 15, 260–67.

7. "The Point of View: 'The Child's Garden'—of Verses and Other Literature," *Scribner's*, April 1896, p. 519. The *Atlantic* also noted the advent of the new genre. In a review of *The One I Knew Best of All*, an anonymous writer observed, "Pierre Loti [(Julien Viaud), author of *A Child's Romance*, available in English in 1891] and Stevenson have set the modern fashion of interpreting the life of the imaginative child in terms which produce not 'juvenile literature,' but books for the big about the little" (June 1894, p. 853). Loti's book is an account of his own boyhood in an austere

Huguenot family in provincial France. He presents himself as a sensitive, dreamy child rather than an inventive, imaginative one. James may have known Loti's book by the time he wrote *Maisie*. I have not found a reference that would indicate this, but his remarks on Loti indicate that he had read many of his books and admired them very much. See "Pierre Loti," *Fortnightly Review*, May 1888, pp. 647–64; *N*, p. 133 (April 1893); *Letters of Henry James*, p. 203 (May 1893); and "London," *Harper's Weekly*, 31 July 1897, p. 754.

   8. "A Cloud of Pinafores," in *More* (London: John Lane, 1899), pp. 179, 172, 173.

   9. Such advertisements ran in nearly all the magazines mentioned in this chapter.

   10. *The Novels of Henry James*, pp. 244–62; quotations taken from pp. 246, 260, and 262.

   11. "Robert Louis Stevenson," *Century*, April 1888, pp. 868–79. Of *A Child's Garden of Verses*, James observes, "The volume is a wonder, for the extraordinary vividness with which it reproduces early impressions; a child might have written it if a child could see childhood from the outside" (p. 871), while *Treasure Island* "embodies a boy's vision of the extraordinary...what we see in it is not only the ideal fable, but...the young reader himself and his state of mind" (p. 877). James also notes "what is peculiar to Mr. Stevenson is that it is his own childhood he appears to delight in. ...[T]here is no strong implication that he is fond of babies; he doesn't speak as a parent, or an uncle, or an educator—he speaks as a contemporary absorbed in his own game" (p. 871).

   12. I have listed the novels that are most relevant to *Maisie*, but it should also be noted that many different kinds of child literature came into existence at the end of the nineteenth century. The child became a subject of interest to psychologists, poets, and essayists, as well as many other novelists. James was undoubtedly acquainted with more than the handful of novels I have named. He might have seen or heard of William Canton's essays and poetry about his daughters, collected as *The Invisible Playmate: A Story of the Unseen* (1894) and *W. V. Her Book, and Various Verses* (1896), since Canton was published in the *Chap-Book* (1 February

1896) and was widely reviewed. James himself reviewed Alice
Meynell's book of essays *The Children* (1897) in his "London"
column in *Harper's Weekly* (6 February 1897), praising her insight.
Both Canton and Meynell stress the sensitivity of children, particularly of little girls; Meynell also deals with the perceptive powers
of children, and some of her insights may have had an influence
on *Maisie*. One further and possibly relevant example of child
literature is Marie Corelli's *The Mighty Atom* (1896). Corelli was a
phenomenally popular lowbrow author whose works might best
be described as a combination of religious tract and romance. *The
Mighty Atom* was written at the height of her fame and was enthusiastically received by all classes of readers. (See *After the Victorians*, pp. 180–86, for an account of Corelli's career.) In it,
Corelli combines the religious tract and the child novel. It is the
story of a child who is raised without religion and who therefore
has no way of explaining the beauty of nature, the death of a
playmate, or the behavior of his mother who deserts him and his
father for another man. This last event, in fact, drives the child to
suicide. It strikes me that *Maisie,* also a story of a child raised
without religion (or "moral sense") and ultimately abandoned by
her parents, is James's answer to Corelli. It is not religion that
saves his child; a capacity for love and an openness to experience
are what matter.

13. "The Point of View: Second Childhood in Literature,"
Scribner's, January 1898, p. 124. Also see Peter Coveney, *The Image of Childhood: A Study of a Theme in English Literature* (1957;
reprint, Harmondsworth, England: Penguin, 1967), pp. 240–79,
for a discussion of the regressive element in late-nineteenth-century child literature.

14. Isle, *Experiments in Form,* praises James's handling of point
of view in the novel, noting that "James's careful tracing of
Maisie's perceptions as the distance gradually narrows between
sensations and understanding is a major achievement in the form
of the novel" (p. 121). Tony Tanner's fine discussion of *Maisie* in
The Reign of Wonder: Naivety and Reality in American Literature
(1965; reprint, New York: Perennial Library, 1967), pp. 278–98,
focuses on Maisie's increasing capacity for reflection or wonder as
it is conveyed through James's handling of point of view in the

book. Both Geismar, *Henry James and the Jacobites,* p. 150, and Wilson, *The Ambiguity of Henry James,* p. 134, find the point of view in the novel voyeuristic.

15. On the contrary, although many contemporary reviewers were offended by the moral squalor of Maisie's surroundings, most spoke favorably of the sweetness and innocence of the child. Some, like James himself in his preface, claimed that the child's perspective redeemed or purified the book. See the reviews in the *Academy,* 16 October 1897, p. 89, and in *Public Opinion,* 30 December 1897, p. 855.

16. That Maisie's sense of the chaos behind life is in fact James's own is confirmed by a rather hysterical notebook entry dated July 1895: "Yesterday at the Borthwicks', at Hampstead, something that Lady Tweedmouth said about the insane frenzy of futile occupation imposed by the London season, added itself to the hideous realization in my own mind—recently so deepened—to suggest that a 'subject' may very well reside in some picture of this overwhelming, self-defeating chaos or cataclysm toward which the whole thing is drifting. The picture residing, exemplified, in the experience of some tremendously exposed and intensely conscious individual—the deluge of people, the insane movement for movement, the ruin of thought, of life, the negation of work, of literature, the swelling, roaring crowds, the 'where are you going?,' the age of Mrs. Jack, the figure of Mrs. Jack, the American, the nightmare—the individual consciousness—the mad, ghastly climax or denouement. It's a splendid subject—if worked round a personal action—situation" (*N,* p. 207). J. A. Ward notes that "This passage...might well serve as 'the germ' for all of James's London fiction" (*The Imagination of Disaster: Evil in the Fiction of Henry James* [Lincoln: University of Nebraska Press, 1961], p. 78).

17. *The One I Knew Best of All: A Memory of the Mind of a Child* (New York: Scribner's, 1893), p. 112. There are some important similarities between *The One I Knew Best of All* and *Maisie* that support my suggestion that James knew this book. Burnett notes that her heroine perceives more than she can articulate (p. 8), that her growth proceeds in discrete episodes (pp. 5, 241), and that her habitual manner is one of apparent passivity and ac-

quiescence (p. 164). The same things are true of Maisie and are as explicitly noted in James's text as they are in Burnett's.

18. *The Search for Form,* pp. 161–62.

19. For a representative sampling, see James W. Gargano, "*What Maisie Knew:* The Evolution of a 'Moral Sense,'" *Nineteenth-Century Fiction* 16 (1961–62): 33–46, who argues that Maisie grows to "self-understanding and moral awareness" (p. 35) and acts idealistically; Joseph A. Hynes, "The Middle Way of Miss Farange: A Study of James's *Maisie,*" *ELH* 32 (1965): 528–53, who argues that Maisie possesses "innate integrity" (p. 551), although her behavior is pragmatic; John C. McCloskey, "What Maisie Knows: A Study of Childhood and Adolescence," *American Literature* 36 (1964–65): 485–513, who argues that Maisie grows selfish and egotistical like her parents; and Edward Wasiolek, "Maisie: Pure or Corrupt?" *College English* 22 (1960–61): 167–72, who notes Maisie's egotism and assertiveness, but like Hynes, argues that she remains uncorrupted by her society.

20. Harris W. Wilson, "What *Did* Maisie Know?" *College English* 17 (1955–56): 279–82, argues that Maisie propositions Sir Claude at the end of the novel in an attempt to keep him, an argument that of course implies that she understands what lovers do. But Wilson bases his argument on "the highly emotional content" (p. 281) of the closing scenes of the book. As my discussion indicates, I agree that these scenes imply an awareness of sexuality, but I see no justification for inferring more.

21. Burnett, *The One I Knew Best of All,* p. 265.

Chapter Seven

1. Critics concerned with social history in relation to *The Awkward Age* are William F. Hall, who in "James's Conception of Society in *The Awkward Age,*" *Nineteenth-Century Fiction* 23 (1968–69): 28–48, discusses the novel as a reflection of contemporary society and as implying an "ideal of society" in which intelligence and sincerity are particularly valued (p. 36); and Elizabeth Owen, who in "'The Awkward Age' and the Contemporary English Scene," *Victorian Studies* 11 (1967–68): 63–82, draws on a wealth

of historical information to show the novel to be a relatively accurate and detailed reflection of its time, and offers a reading of the novel in which she concludes that James's final stance is one of "detached, complex irony" rather than affirmation of any positive values (p. 79). Owen also notes James's familiarity with E. F. Benson's dialogue novel *Dodo*. She observes that "James ...was always ready to consider public taste, provided he could turn out a first-quality article" and suggests that the tight structure of *The Awkward Age* was James's attempt to "stiffen a slack popular genre" (p. 65).

2. Clarence Rook, "Anthony Hope," *Chap-Book*, 15 March 1897, p. 355, describes the evolution of the dialogue novel from the weekly periodical feature, although he mistakenly assumes that *Black and White* ran the first dialogues.

3. *The Awkward Age* was serialized in *Harper's Weekly* from October 1898 to January 1899.

4. A confirmatory sign of the popularity of dialogue was its use for serious topics. Vernon Lee used it to present her views on philosophical and social issues in *Baldwin: Being Dialogues on Views and Aspirations* (1886) and in *Althea: A Second Book of Dialogues on Aspirations and Duties* (1894). James, too, used the form for presenting his ideas on literary and social issues in "After the Play" and "An Animated Conversation."

5. Cruse, *After the Victorians*, pp. 186–88, discusses *Dodo* as a roman à clef. Margot Asquith, *The Autobiography of Margot Asquith*, ed. Mark Bonham Carter (Cambridge, Mass.: Houghton Mifflin, 1962), pp. 117–53, gives an account of the "Souls." The account includes a letter from James to Margot Asquith commenting on a diary that she had sent him: she had shed light, he says, on a group of people he had watched with interest from the outside (p. 152).

6. *Our Family Affairs: 1867–1896* (London: Cassell, 1920), p. 282. In spite of James's reservations, *Dodo* was popular enough to merit Benson's writing an additional Dodo dialogue, ironically called "The Taming of Dodo," printed in the *Chap-Book*, 15 May 1897, pp. 11–16, an issue that included two chapters of James's *Maisie*.

7. Cruse, *After the Victorians*, p. 189.

8. *Letters of Henry James,* p. 333 (1899).

9. Ian Gregor, "The Novel of Moral Consciousness: 'The Awkward Age' (1899)," in *The Moral and the Story,* by Ian Gregor and Brian Nicholas (London: Faber & Faber, 1962), pp. 151–84, offers a fine discussion of this aspect of the novel. He shows how the characters who are a part of London society in the book use a language which is divorced from moral values and as a result think of other people as objects to be manipulated. Margaret Walters, "Keeping the Place Tidy for the Young Female Mind: *The Awkward Age,*" in *The Air of Reality: New Essays on Henry James,* ed. John Goode (London: Methuen, 1972), pp. 190–218, shows how all the characters, through both their language and their behavior, are a part of their society and concludes that James "no longer tries to envision a non-social self" (p. 217). Isle, *Experiments in Form,* pp. 165–204, shows how the symmetrical form of the novel and the extensive use of dialogue effectively portray a sterile society in which talk has replaced action.

10. "Gyp's" heroines, in contrast, are rather pleasant women but are not particularly clever. The heroine of her widely popular and many times translated *Chiffon's Marriage* (1894; first English trans. 1895) is a representative example. As my discussion of James will suggest, he seems to have responded to specific elements in the English versions of the dialogue novel and the New Woman novel in writing *The Awkward Age.*

11. The conflict between mothers and their "revolting daughters" was a subject of widespread interest in the nineties. This topical issue also entered into the composition of *The Awkward Age,* in, as I will indicate, an unusual form. Hamlin Hill, "'The Revolt of the Daughters': A Suggested Source for 'The Awkward Age,'" *Notes and Queries* 206 (1961): 347–49, notes the likelihood of James's knowledge of contemporary magazine articles dealing with the behavior and roles of mothers and daughters.

12. *The Maiden's Progress* (New York: Harper, 1894), p. 166.

13. "Life and Letters," *Harper's Weekly,* 4 May 1895, p. 417. Also see Lloyd Fernando, "The Radical Ideology of the 'New Woman,'" *Southern Review: An Australian Journal of Literary Studies* 2 (1967): "Many problem-novelists, enamoured of the 'advanced' implications of the woman's movement, rapidly sacrificed the

artistic potential of the novel as a literary form for the sake of illustrating particular views or theses on such topics as woman's role in society, the double standard of morality, and free love. The characterisation of the 'New Woman' suffered most" (p. 217).

14. Colby, *The Singular Anomaly,* p. 61.

15. "London," *Harper's Weekly,* 21 August 1897, p. 834. James is deploring the inappropriate use of classical references and he comments on the "strange colloquies in which Euripides gives an arm to Sarah Grand." I am not sure what he is referring to. In *The Heavenly Twins,* however, there is some discussion of the disregard the classical authors, including Euripides, had for women, and the name "Evadne" is from Euripides' play *The Suppliants.*

16. Colby, p. 22.

17. *The Story of an African Farm* (1883; reprint, Harmondsworth, England: Penguin, 1971), p. 180.

18. *The New Woman: In Haste and at Leisure* (New York: Merriam, 1895), p. 315.

19. See George Gissing, *The Odd Women,* 1893, and Grant Allen, *The Woman Who Did,* 1895.

20. Krook, *The Ordeal of Consciousness,* pp. 135–66, also deals with Nanda's victimization. She attributes Nanda's situation to her social milieu and does not single out Mrs. Brook, as I do, as a particularly harmful influence.

21. *The Treacherous Years,* p. 259. Edel continues: "For this was the androgynous nature of the creator and the drama of his novels: innocence and worldliness, the paradisiacal America and the cruel and corrupt Europe—or in other variations, youthful ignorant America and wise and civilized Europe."

22. *Critic,* August 1899, p. 755.

Epilogue

1. James, "The Art of Fiction," p. 506.

2. *Lippincott's,* February 1887, p. 359.

3. *Literary World,* 11 December 1897, p. 454.

4. Although *The Sacred Fount* was not inspired by previous best sellers, it is not as remote from the world of the best seller as

modern readers might think. The review in the *Athenaeum* (2 March 1901, p. 272) discusses James's portrayal of the contemporary "smart set" in the novel. And the novel itself resembles another book on the same subject: Elinor Glyn's extremely popular *The Visits of Elizabeth* (1900), the story of a debutante who visits at a number of fashionable country houses and, to the embarrassment and amusement of her elders, sees too much and asks too many questions.

5. Henry Nash Smith, *Democracy and the Novel: Popular Resistance to Classic American Writers* (New York: Oxford University Press, 1978), pp. 150–61, traces the emergence of this new reading public as it was reflected in the critical reception of James's novels.

6. *Letters of Henry James,* p. 135 (1888).

WORKS CITED

Allen, Grant. "The Pot Boiler." *Longman's,* October 1892, pp. 591–602.

Altick, Richard D. *The English Common Reader: A Social History of the Mass Reading Public 1800–1900.* 1957. Reprint. Chicago: University of Chicago Press, Phoenix Books, 1963.

Asquith, Margot. *The Autobiography of Margot Asquith.* Edited by Mark Bonham Carter. Cambridge, Mass.: Houghton Mifflin, 1962. (Abridged version of the 1920–22 edition.)

Banta, Martha. *Henry James and the Occult: The Great Extension.* Bloomington: Indiana University Press, 1972.

Barzun, Jacques. "Henry James, Melodramatist." *Kenyon Review* 5 (1943). Reprinted in *The Question of Henry James: A Collection of Critical Essays,* edited by F. W. Dupee. New York: Henry Holt & Co., 1945, pp. 254–66.

Beer, Thomas. *The Mauve Decade: American Life at the End of the Nineteenth Century.* 1926. Reprint. New York: Random House, Vintage Books, 1961.

Beerbohm, Max. "A Cloud of Pinafores." In *More.* London: John Lane, 1899, pp. 169–81.

———. "Enoch Soames." In *Seven Men.* London: William Heinemann, 1919, pp. 1–48.

Bennett, Arnold. *Fame and Fiction: An Enquiry into Certain Popularities.* London: Grant Richards, 1901.

Benson, E. F. *Our Family Affairs: 1867–1896.* London: Cassell, 1920.

———. "The Taming of Dodo." *Chap-Book,* 15 May 1897, pp. 11–16.

Besant, Walter. "The Art of Fiction: A Lecture Delivered at the Royal Institution, April 25, 1884." In *The Art of Fiction,* by Walter Besant and Henry James. Boston: DeWolfe, Fiske, 1884, pp. 3–43.

———. *The Pen and The Book.* London: Thomas Burleigh, 1899.

Black, William. *Macleod of Dare.* 3 vols. London: Macmillan, 1878.

Brooks, Peter. *The Melodramatic Imagination: Balzac, Henry James, Melodrama, and the Mode of Excess.* New Haven: Yale University Press, 1976.

Buchanan, Robert. *The Martyrdom of Madelaine.* 3 vols. London: Chatto & Windus, 1882.

——. "The Modern Young Man as Critic." *Universal Review,* March 1889, pp. 353–72.

Buckley, Jerome Hamilton. *The Victorian Temper: A Study in Literary Culture.* 1951. Reprint. New York: Random House, Vintage Books, 1964.

Buitenhuis, Peter. *The Grasping Imagination: The American Writings of Henry James.* Toronto: University of Toronto Press, 1970.

Burnett, Frances Hodgson. *The One I Knew Best of All: A Memory of the Mind of a Child.* New York: Scribner's, 1893.

Cargill, Oscar. *The Novels of Henry James.* 1961. Reprint. New York: Hafner, 1971.

Colby, Vineta. *The Singular Anomaly: Woman Novelists of the Nineteenth Century.* 1970. Reprint. New York: New York University Press, 1972.

Coveny, Peter. *The Image of Childhood: A Study of a Theme in English Literature.* 1957. Reprint. Harmondsworth, England: Penguin, 1967.

Crawford, F. Marion. *The Novel: What It Is.* New York: Macmillan, 1893.

Cruse, Amy. *After the Victorians.* London: George Allen & Unwin, 1938.

——. *The Victorians and Their Reading.* 1935. Reprint. Boston: Houghton Mifflin, 1936.

Davidson, John. *The North Wall.* Glasgow: Wilson & McCormick, 1885.

Davis, Sara deSaussure. "Feminist Sources in *The Bostonians.*" *American Literature* 50 (1978–79): 570–87.

Du Maurier, George. Cartoon: "Maudle on the Choice of a Profession." *Punch,* 12 February 1881, p. 62.

——. Cartoon: "Where the Shoe Pinches." *Punch,* 4 December 1880, p. 258.

Dupee, F. W. *Henry James*. 1951. Reprint. Garden City, N.J.: Doubleday, 1956.

Edel, Leon. "Henry James: The Dramatic Years." In *Guy Domville*, by Henry James, edited by Leon Edel. 1949. Reprint. Philadelphia: Lippincott, Keystone Books, 1960, pp. 13–121.

——. *Henry James: The Middle Years, 1882–1895*. Philadelphia: Lippincott, 1962.

——. *Henry James: The Treacherous Years, 1895–1901*. Philadelphia: Lippincott, 1969.

"Editor's Easy Chair: Modern Ghosts." *Harper's*, September 1890, pp. 635–37.

Ferguson, Alfred R. "The Triple Quest of Henry James: Fame, Art, and Fortune." *American Literature* 27 (1955–56): 475–98.

Fergusson, Francis. *The Idea of a Theater, a Study of Ten Plays; The Art of Drama in a Changing Perspective*. 1949. Reprint. Garden City, N.J.: Doubleday, Anchor Books, n.d. [1954].

Fernando, Lloyd. "The Radical Ideology of the 'New Woman.'" *Southern Review: An Australian Journal of Literary Studies* 2 (1967): 206–22.

Fetterley, Judith. *The Resisting Reader: A Feminist Approach to American Fiction*. Bloomington: Indiana University Press, 1978.

Flexner, Eleanor. *Century of Struggle: The Woman's Rights Movement in the United States*. 1959. Reprint. New York: Atheneum, 1973.

Gard, Roger, ed. *Henry James: The Critical Heritage*. London: Routledge & Kegan Paul, 1968.

Gargano, James W. "*What Maisie Knew:* The Evolution of a 'Moral Sense.'" *Nineteenth-Century Fiction* 16 (1961–62): 33–46.

Geismar, Maxwell. *Henry James and the Jacobites*. 1962. Reprint. New York: Hill & Wang, 1965.

Gissing, George. *Workers in the Dawn*. 2 vols. 1880. Reprint. New York: Doubleday Doran, 1935.

Goode, John. "The Art of Fiction: Walter Besant and Henry James." In *Tradition and Toleration in Nineteenth-Century Fiction: Critical Essays on Some English and American Novels*, edited by

David Howard, John Lucas, and John Goode. London: Routledge & Kegan Paul, 1966, pp. 243–81.

Gordon, D. J., and John Stokes. "The Reference of *The Tragic
Muse.*" In *The Air of Reality: New Essays on Henry James,* edited
by John Goode. London: Methuen, 1972, pp. 80–167.

Gosse, Edmund. *Aspects and Impressions.* London: Cassell, 1922.

Graham, Kenneth. *Henry James: The Drama of Fulfillment.*
London: Oxford University Press, Clarendon Press, 1975.

Greene, Graham. "Henry James: The Private Universe." In *The
English Novelists,* edited by Derek Verschoyle, 1936. Reprinted
in *The Lost Childhood and Other Essays.* New York: Viking, 1952,
pp. 21–30.

———. "Henry James: The Religious Aspect." In *Contemporary
Essays, 1933,* edited by Sylva Norman, 1933. Reprinted in *The
Lost Childhood and Other Essays.* New York: Viking, 1952,
pp. 31–39.

Gregor, Ian. "The Novel of Moral Consciousness: 'The Awkward
Age' (1899)." In *The Moral and the Story,* by Ian Gregor and
Brian Nicholas. London: Faber & Faber, 1962, pp. 151–84.

Hall, Willliam F. "James's Conception of Society in *The Awkward
Age.*" *Nineteenth-Century Fiction* 23 (1968–69): 28–48.

Harlow, Virginia. *Thomas Sergeant Perry: A Biography and Letters to
Perry from William, Henry, and Garth Wilkinson James.* Durham,
N.C.: Duke University Press, 1950.

Hart, James D. *The Popular Book: A History of America's Literary
Taste.* 1950. Reprint. Berkeley: University of California Press,
1963.

Hill, Hamlin. "'The Revolt of the Daughters': A Suggested
Source for 'The Awkward Age.'" *Notes and Queries* 206 (1961):
347–49.

Howard, David. "The Bostonians." In *The Air of Reality: New Essays on Henry James,* edited by John Goode. London: Methuen,
1972, pp. 60–80.

Howe, Irving. Introduction to *The Bostonians,* by Henry James.
New York: Random House, Modern Library, 1956, pp. v–
xxviii.

———. "The Political Vocation." In *Politics and the Novel,* 1957.
Reprinted in *Henry James: A Collection of Critical Essays,* edited

by Leon Edel. Englewood Cliffs, N.J.: Prentice-Hall, 1963, pp. 156–71.

[Howells, William Dean]. "Editor's Study." Review of *The Princess Casamassima*, by Henry James. *Harper's*, April 1887, p. 829.

Howells, William Dean. "Life and Letters." *Harper's Weekly*, 4 May 1895, pp. 416–17.

Hunt, Violet. *The Maiden's Progress*. New York: Harper, 1894.

Hynes, Joseph A. "The Middle Way of Miss Farange: A Study of James's *Maisie*." *ELH* 32 (1965): 528–53.

Hynes, Samuel. *The Edwardian Turn of Mind*. Princeton: Princeton University Press, 1968.

Isle, Walter. *Experiments in Form: Henry James's Novels, 1896–1901*. Cambridge, Mass.: Harvard University Press, 1968.

Jackson, Holbrook. *The Eighteen Nineties: A Review of Art and Ideas at the Close of the Nineteenth Century*. 1913. Reprint. New York: Capricorn, 1966.

James, Henry. "After the Play." *New Review*, June 1889, pp. 30–46.

——. "American Letter." *Literature*, 11 June 1898, pp. 676–78.

——. "An Animated Conversation." *Scribner's*, March 1889, pp. 371–84.

——. "The Art of Fiction." *Longman's*, September 1884, pp. 502–21.

——. *The Bostonians*. New York: Random House, Modern Library, 1956.

——. *The Complete Plays of Henry James*. Edited by Leon Edel. Philadelphia: Lippincott, 1949.

——. "Du Maurier and London Society." *Century*, May 1883, pp. 48–65.

——. *Henry James: Letters*. Vol. 2. Edited by Leon Edel. Cambridge, Mass.: Harvard University Press, 1975.

——. Introduction to *Soldiers Three*, by Rudyard Kipling. Leipzig: Heinemann & Balestier, 1891, pp. [i]–xxi.

——. *The Letters of Henry James*. Vol. 1. Edited by Percy Lubbock. New York: Scribner's, 1920.

——. "London." In *Essays in London and Elsewhere*. New York: Harper, 1893, pp. 1–43.

——. "London." *Harper's Weekly*, 6 February 1897, pp. 134–35.

———. "London." *Harper's Weekly,* 31 July 1897, p. 754.

———. "London." *Harper's Weekly,* 21 August 1897, p. 834.

———. *The Notebooks of Henry James.* Edited by F. O. Matthiessen and Kenneth B. Murdock. 1947. Reprint. New York: Oxford University Press, 1961.

———. *The Novels and Tales of Henry James.* 26 vols. 1907–17. Reprint. New York: Scribner's, 1961–65.

———. "On the Occasion of Hedda Gabler." *New Review,* June 1891, pp. 519–30.

———. "Pierre Loti." *Fortnightly Review,* May 1888, pp. 647–64.

———. *The Princess Casamassima.* 3 vols. London: Macmillan, 1886.

[———]. Review of *Macleod of Dare,* by William Black. *Nation,* 19 December 1878, pp. 387–88.

———. "Robert Louis Stevenson." *Century,* April 1888, pp. 868–79.

———. *Selected Letters of Henry James.* Edited by Leon Edel. London: Rupert Hart-Davis, 1956.

Jerome, Jerome K. *Told after Supper.* London: Leadenhall Press, 1891.

Keating, P. J. *The Working Classes in Victorian Fiction.* London: Routledge & Kegan Paul, 1971.

Kerr, Howard. *Mediums, and Spirit-Rappers, and Roaring Radicals: Spiritualism in American Literature, 1850–1900.* Urbana: University of Illinois Press, 1972.

Krook, Dorothea. *The Ordeal of Consciousness in Henry James.* 1962. Reprint. Cambridge: Cambridge University Press, 1967.

Leavis, Q. D. *Fiction and the Reading Public.* 1932. Reprint. New York: Russell & Russell, 1965.

Lee, Vernon [Violet Paget]. *Miss Brown.* 1884. Reprint. New York: George Munroe, Seaside Library, n.d.

Levy, Leo. *Versions of Melodrama: A Study of the Fiction and Drama of Henry James, 1865–1897.* Berkeley: University of California Press, 1957.

Linton, Eliza Lynn. *The New Women: In Haste and at Leisure.* New York: Merriam, 1895.

Lively, Robert A. *Fiction Fights the Civil War: An Unfinished Chapter in the Literary History of the American People.* Chapel Hill: University of North Carolina Press, 1957.

Long, Robert Emmet. *The Great Succession: Henry James and the Legacy of Hawthorne.* Pittsburgh: University of Pittsburgh Press, 1979.

Lovecraft, Howard Phillips. *Supernatural Horror in Literature.* 1927. Reprint. New York: Dover, 1973.

McCloskey, John C. "What Maisie Knows: A Study of Childhood and Adolescence." *American Literature* 36 (1964–65): 485–513.

Martin, Jay. *Harvests of Change: American Literature 1865–1914.* Englewood Cliffs, N.J.: Prentice-Hall, 1967.

Matthiessen, F. O. *The James Family Including Selections from the Writings of Henry James, Senior, William, Henry, and Alice James.* 1947. Reprint. New York: Knopf, 1961.

Monteiro, George. *Henry James and John Hay: The Record of a Friendship.* 1963. Reprint. Providence: Brown University Press, 1965.

Moore, George. *Confessions of a Young Man.* Edited by Susan Dick. Montreal: McGill-Queen's University Press, 1972.

Mott, Frank Luther. *Golden Multitudes: The Story of Best Sellers in the United States.* New York: Macmillan, 1947.

"Mr. Henry James." *Murray's,* November 1891, pp. 641–54.

O'Neill, John P. *Workable Design: Action and Situation in the Fiction of Henry James.* Port Washington, N.Y.: Kennikat Press, 1973.

Owen, Elizabeth. "'The Awkward Age' and the Contemporary English Scene." *Victorian Studies* 11 (1967–68): 63–82.

Penzoldt, Peter. *The Supernatural in Fiction.* 1952. Reprint. New York: Humanities Press, 1965.

Perosa, Sergio. *Henry James and the Experimental Novel.* Charlottesville: University of Virginia Press, 1978.

"The Point of View: 'The Child's Garden'—of Verses and Other Literature." *Scribner's,* April 1896, pp. 519–20.

"The Point of View: Second Childhood in Literature." *Scribner's,* January 1898, pp. 123–24.

Poole, Adrian. *Gissing in Context.* London: Macmillan, 1975.

Powers, Lyall H. *Henry James and the Naturalist Movement.* East Lansing: Michigan State University Press, 1971.

Rahv, Philip. Introduction to *The Bostonians,* by Henry James. New York: Dial Press, 1945, pp. v–ix.

"Recent American Fiction." *Atlantic,* January 1885, pp. 121–32.

Review of *The Awkward Age,* by Henry James. *Critic,* August 1899, pp. 754–56.

Review of *The Bostonians,* by Henry James. *Literary World,* 17 April 1886, p. 137.

Review of *The Bostonians,* by Henry James. *Nation,* 13 May 1886, pp. 407–08.

Review of *The One I Knew Best of All,* by Pierre Loti (Julien Viaud). *Atlantic,* June 1894, p. 853.

Review of *The Other House,* by Henry James. *Critic,* 28 November 1896, p. 335.

Review of *The Other House,* by Henry James. *Saturday Review,* 31 October 1896, pp. 474–75.

Review of *The Princess Casamassima,* by Henry James. *Lippincott's,* February 1887, p. 359.

Review of *The Sacred Fount,* by Henry James. *Athenaeum,* 2 March 1901, p. 272.

Review of *The Tragic Muse,* by Henry James. *Athenaeum,* 26 July 1890, p. 124.

Review of *The Tragic Muse,* by Henry James. *Public Opinion,* 13 September 1890, pp. 539–40.

Review of *What Maisie Knew,* by Henry James. *Academy,* 16 October 1897, p. 89.

Review of *What Maisie Knew,* by Henry James. *Literary World,* 11 December 1897, pp. 454–55.

Review of *What Maisie Knew,* by Henry James. *Public Opinion,* 30 December 1897, p. 855.

Roe, E. P. *An Original Belle.* 1885. Reprint. New York: Collier, 1902.

Roellinger, Francis X. "Psychical Research and 'The Turn of the Screw.'" *American Literature* 20 (1948–49). Reprinted in *The Turn of the Screw: An Authoritative Text, Backgrounds and Sources, Essays in Criticism,* edited by Robert Kimbrough. New York: Norton, 1966, pp. 132–42.

Rook, Clarence. "Anthony Hope." *Chap-Book,* 15 March 1897, pp. 354–56.

Scarborough, Dorothy. *The Supernatural in Modern English Fiction.* New York: Putnam's, 1917.

Schreiner, Olive. *The Story of an African Farm.* 1883. Reprint. Harmondsworth, England: Penguin, 1971.

[Scudder, H. E.] "James, Crawford, and Howells." *Atlantic,* June 1886, pp. 850–57.

Sheppard, E. A. *Henry James and "The Turn of the Screw."* Auckland: Auckland University Press, 1974.

Sinclair, Andrew. *The Emancipation of the American Woman.* 1965. Reprint. New York: Harper & Row, Colophon, 1966.

Smith, Henry Nash. *Democracy and the Novel: Popular Resistance to Classic American Writers.* New York: Oxford University Press, 1978.

Smith, Herbert F., and Michael Peinovich. "*The Bostonians:* Creation and Revision." *Bulletin of the New York Public Library* 73 (1969): 298–308.

Smith, Janet Adam, ed. *Henry James and Robert Louis Stevenson: A Record of Friendship and Criticism.* London: Rupert Hart-Davis, 1948.

Spilka, Mark. "Henry James and Walter Besant: 'The Art of Fiction' Controversy." *Novel* 6 (1972–73): 101–19.

Stone, Donald David. *Novelists in a Changing World: Meredith, James, and the Transformation of English Fiction in the 1880's.* Cambridge, Mass.: Harvard University Press, 1972.

Stone, Edward. *The Battle and the Books: Some Aspects of Henry James.* Athens: Ohio University Press, 1964.

Tanner, Tony. *The Reign of Wonder: Naivety and Reality in American Literature.* 1965. Reprint. New York: Perennial Library, 1967.

Taylor, John Russell. *The Rise and Fall of the Well-Made Play.* London: Methuen, 1967.

Tilley, W. H. *The Background of "The Princess Casamassima."* Gainesville: University of Florida Press, 1961.

Tinter, Adeline R. "Henry James Criticism: A Current Perspective." *American Literary Realism: 1870–1910* 7 (1974): 158–68.

Tomsich, John. *A Genteel Endeavor: American Culture and Politics in the Gilded Age.* Stanford, Calif.: Stanford University Press, 1971.

"Topics of the Time: Battles and Leaders of the Civil War." *Century,* October 1884, pp. 943–44.

Trilling, Lionel. Introduction to *The Bostonians,* by Henry James. London: Lehmann, 1952, pp. vii–xv.

———. *"The Princess Casamassima."* In *The Liberal Imagination: Essays on Literature and Society.* 1950. Reprint. New York: Doubleday, Anchor Books, 1953, pp. 55–88.

Veeder, William, *Henry James—the Lessons of the Master: Popular Fiction and Personal Style in the Nineteenth Century.* Chicago: University of Chicago Press, 1975.

Walters, Margaret. "Keeping the Place Tidy for the Young Female Mind: *The Awkward Age.*" In *The Air of Reality: New Essays on Henry James,* edited by John Goode. London: Methuen, 1972, pp. 190–218.

Ward, Mrs. Humphry. *Miss Bretherton.* London: Macmillan, 1884.

Ward, J. A. *The Imagination of Disaster: Evil in the Fiction of Henry James.* Lincoln: University of Nebraska Press, 1961.

———. *The Search for Form: Studies in the Structure of James's Fiction.* Chapel Hill: University of North Carolina Press, 1967.

Wasiolek, Edward. "Maisie: Pure or Corrupt?" *College English* 22 (1960–61): 167–72.

Wasserstrom, William. *Heiress of all the Ages: Sex and Sentiment in the Genteel Tradition.* Minneapolis: University of Minnesota Press, 1959.

Webb, Beatrice. *My Apprenticeship.* 1926. Reprint. Harmondsworth, England: Penguin, 1971.

Wedgwood, Julia. Review of *The Princess Casamassima,* by Henry James. *Contemporary Review,* December 1886, pp. 899–901.

Wells, H. G. *The Country of the Blind and Other Stories.* London: Thomas Nelson, n.d. [1911].

———. "The Red Room." *Chap-Book,* 15 February 1896, pp. 314–24.

Wiesenfarth, Joseph. *Henry James and the Dramatic Analogy: A Study of the Major Novels of the Middle Period.* New York: Fordham University Press, 1963.

Williams, Raymond. *The Long Revolution.* 1961. Reprint. Harmondsworth, England: Penguin, 1975.

Wilson, Edmund. "The Ambiguity of Henry James." *Hound and Horn* 7 (1933–34). Reprinted with revisions and additions of 1938, 1948, and 1959 in *A Casebook on Henry James's "The Turn of the Screw,*" edited by Gerald Willen. 2d ed. New York: Crowell, 1969, pp. 115–53.

Wilson, Harris W. "What *Did* Maisie Know?" *College English* 17 (1955–56): 279–82.

Ziff, Larzer. *The American 1890's: Life and Times of a Lost Generation.* 1966. Reprint. New York: Viking, 1968.

INDEX